# Building Solo Lines From Cells
## (for all instruments)

### by
### Randy Vincent

Cover artwork by Sueann Bettison Sher
Cover design by Linda McLaughlin
Music engraving by Larry Dunlap

# TABLE OF CONTENTS

# Preface

This book is for all instruments but is actually an edited version of my last book "Jazz Guitar Soloing: The Cellular Approach," which is very guitar-specific. Jamey Abersold suggested that it could be valuable for all musicians and thus the new edited version that eliminates guitar strings and fingerings that are not necessary for other instruments. The examples are in concert pitch but sound one octave lower as in written guitar music—but any octave is good depending on the range and register of your chosen instrument. For horn players, I suggest working out the examples on piano first, then transpose to your horn, preferably without having to write them out. This will prove valuable when doing some examples based on stock tunes and things based on rhythm changes, Coltrane changes, etc.

The concept for the book is based on the idea that any long line transcribed from any great jazz solo can be broken down into many smaller "cells" that have melodic content that are so idiomatic to the jazz language that they can be recombined into new individual lines that sound as authentic as the original without being a mere regurgitation of part of someone else's solo. Since the book was originally for guitarists many of the transcribed lines are from guitarists such as Wes Montgomery, Joe Pass, Pat Martino, etc. but also many from other great instrumentalists as well, including Miles Davis, McCoy Tyner, and Michael Brecker, among others.

Let me leave you with a thought on HOW to practice in order to get the maximum benefit from the exercises in this book:

It's a good idea to break things down and practice small amounts with focus on the fine details, and don't worry that it seems there's too much you're not getting to. Patience is key. If you chip away on bite-size pieces they will eventually accumulate into a vast amount of useful material. Take your time and make sure you hear all the notes intended and only the notes intended—and evenly in time. Don't worry about the other patterns you're not getting to yet. There will be plenty of other days for those.

Randy Vincent

# Chapter 1 – Cycles and II-V Sequences

Let's explore "cellular" improvisation as a concept in itself. Actually, almost any long line of notes could be sliced up into short melodic cells which can be used separately and re-combined into other long lines. When jazz musicians refer to melodic cells, they are most commonly four-note cells. Hal Galper in his great book *Forward Motion* defines a cell as a four-note group with at least three of the notes being chord tones. Jerry Bergonzi uses a similar concept. Most of the cells we'll use in this book will fit that description, although later there will be some other types as well.

Four-note cells are not only useful for re-combining into long lines over a given chord, but are especially useful for improvising lines over very fast-moving changes. Four-note cells played as eighth-notes only last for only two beats, so changes that last for only two beats each are perfect for some cellular work-outs. These could include fast-moving cycles, quick II-V sequences, various turnarounds, "Coltrane changes" (as in "Giant Steps") and more. Let's get started with some fast-moving dominant cycles.

## Fast-moving dominant cycles

A dominant cycle is a progression of all dominant 7th type chords moving counter-clockwise around the the circle of fifths (each new root being down-a-fifth or up-a-fourth from the previous root). The bridge of "Rhythm Changes" is a dominant cycle, but the chords last for two whole measures each, or eight beats apiece. Right now we want to check out changes lasting only two beats each, so we'll specify them as "fast-moving" dominant cycles.

*Some actual examples of fast-moving dominant cycles*
Play Ex.1-1, from a recording of an improvised solo by Joe Pass.

Notice that each cell begins on the root of each chord. The first three chords use an ascending sequence, the root, 2nd, 3rd, and 5th of each chord. This pattern is very common and will be identified as the 1-2-3-5 cell from now on. The Ab7 chord uses a descending pattern going right down the scale (1-b7-6-5). The Db7 chord has the same descending scale notes, but the order has been changed to make a nice phrase ending (1-5-6-b7). In the first three chords the three chord tones are root, 3rd, and 5th, with one passing tone, the 2nd. In the descending patterns the three chord tones are root, b7th, and 5th, with one passing note, the 6th.

Cells that start on the root and end on the 5th lead to the root of each following chord, so they can form sequences that go "root to root".

Now check out ex.1-2, from a little later in the same solo.

This time each cell begins on the 3rd of each chord. The line alternates between two cell variations to form an eight-note sequence. All the cells consist of 3rd, b9th, root, and b7th. This pattern is also very common and from now on will be referred to as the 3-b9-1-b7 cell. The variations are created by changing between leaping up from the 3rd to the b9th, or descending scale-wise from the 3rd to the b9th. All four notes of each cell are chord tones on a dom7b9 chord, but can also be used on straight dom7 chords with three chord tones and the b9th acting as a passing tone.

Cells that start on the 3rd and end on the b7th lead to the 3rd of each following chord, so they can form sequences that go "3rd to 3rd".

Ex.1-3 was transcribed from another Joe Pass solo. The Gmi7 is just a lead-in to the dominant cycle, which starts at the C7.

This time Joe uses a four beat sequence that alternates between cells beginning on the 5th and the 3rd of the dom7 chords. The exception is the last chord, Db7, where a surprise #11 replaces the 3rd. The cells starting on the 5th are descending dom7 arpeggios, 5-3-1-b7, all chord tones. The cells starting on the 3rd are ascending 3-5-b7-9 arpeggios, again all chord tones.

Ex.1-4 is also from Joe.

Each cell begins on the 3rd of each chord, but two new cells are used this time. On the G7 and the Bb7 the cell is 3-2-1-b7, while on the C7 and the F7 the cell is 3-5-1-b7. The descending cell is scale-wise with three chord tones, 3rd, root, and b7th, with one passing tone, the 2nd. The ascending cell is an arpeggio permutation, all chord tones. Notice that this is another "3rd to 3rd" sequence, connected by the b7ths.

Ex.1-5 is once again from Joe Pass.

This example reveals an interesting fact: when descending scale-wise from a chord tone in eighth notes in a fast-moving dominant cycle, you land on the same chord tone on each successive chord.

I'm going to start by showing exercises based on these examples, if only because these are the examples I first studied and these are the exercises I first used to gain fluency on fast-moving cycles. Later we'll expand the vocabulary further.

# "Root to root" cycles

## *"Root to root" cycles – one bar sequences*

Ex.1-6 shows a "root to root" cycle using one ascending 1-2-3-5 cell followed by one descending 1-b7-6-5 cell, forming a one measure pattern that forms a descending sequence. Only the first two bars are shown. Start high on your instrument and continue the exercise as far down as practical.

## *"Root to root" cycles – two bar sequences*

Ex.1-7 shows a "root to root" cycle using two ascending 1-2-3-5 cells followed by two descending 1-b7-6-5 cells, forming a two measure pattern that results in a decending sequence. Only the first two and a half bars are shown. Start high on your instrument and continue the exercise as far down as practical.

## *"Root to root" cycles – descending full range followed by ascending full range*

Ex.1-8 connects the descending root-oriented patterns full range followed by the ascending root-oriented patterns full range.

Ex.1-9 shows another version, starting and ending with ascending patterns.

4

With these in combination with our previous examples you could play never-ending root-oriented cycles from any location on your instrument, up or down as far as range allows before having to reverse direction.

## "3rd to 3rd" cycles

### *"3rd to 3rd" cycles – one bar sequences*

Ex.1-10 shows a "3rd to 3rd" cycle using one ascending 3-5-1-b7 cell followed by one descending 3-2-1-b7 cell, forming a one measure pattern that forms a descending sequence. Only the first two bars are shown. Start high and continue the exercise as far down as practical.

### *"3rd to 3rd" cycles – two bar sequences*

Using the root-oriented exercises as a model, work out the two bar sequences.

### *"3rd to 3rd" cycles – descending across the entire range, then ascending*

Ex.1-11 connects the descending 3rd-oriented patterns full range followed by the ascending 3rd-oriented patterns full range.

Ex.1-12 shows another version, starting and ending with ascending patterns. With these in combination with our previous examples you could play never-ending 3rd-oriented cycles from any location on your instrument.

*3rd-oriented dom7b9 cycles – one bar sequences*

Ex.1-13 shows a "3rd to 3rd" pattern using a b9th on each chord, as demonstrated by Joe Pass in Ex.1-2. This one bar sequence descends in whole steps.

*3rd-oriented dom7b9 cycles – descending across the entire range*
*followed by ascending across the entire range*

Ex.1-14 connects the descending 3-b9-1-b7 patterns all the way across the entire range followed by the ascending 3-b9-1-b7 patterns all the way across the entire range.

*3rd-oriented dom7b9 cycles*

Ex.1-15 shows another version, starting and ending with ascending patterns. With these in combination with our previous examples you can play never-ending 3rd-oriented dom7b9 cycles from any location on your instrument.

## "3rd to 5th" cycles

*"3rd to 5th" cycles – one bar sequences*

Now let's check out a pattern that goes back and forth between cells that start on the 3rd and cells that start on the 5th, inspired by the Joe Pass line from ex.1-3. The 3-5-b7-9 cell alternates with the 5-3-1-b7 cell. This automatically creates one bar sequences. Since these sequences alternate between cells with different starting notes, they don't lend themselves to all the same sequences we've been using, although we can form some two bar sequences through the use of octave displacements.

*"3rd to 5th" cycles – two bar sequences using octave displacements*

Ex.1-16 shows a two bar sequence of the "3rd to 5th" cycle using octave displacements.

This last example shows that arpeggio permutations can be used as cells to connect to different starting notes for the chords in fast-moving cycles. Let's explore that concept further to expand on our Joe Pass inspired cycles.

## "3rd to root" cycles

*"3rd to root" cycles – one bar sequences*

Ex.1-17 is a pattern that goes back and forth between cells that start on the 3rd and cells that start on the root. The descending cell is an inverted arpeggio permutation, 3-1-b7-5 (all chord tones). The ascending cell is another arpeggio, 1-3-5-b7 (again, all chord tones). This back-and-forth pattern automatically generates a one bar sequence.

*"3rd to root" cycles using octave displacements*

Ex.1-18 shows a one bar sequence using octave displacements with the "3rd to root" cycle.

## Fast-moving cycle connections in a nutshell

To help us expand further, let's briefly analyze the connections we've been using. Let's look at one measure examples using G7-C7 resolving to F7.

The "3rd to root" cycle we just looked at is demonstrated in Ex.1-19. Ex.1-19A shows 3-1-b7-5 descending going to 1-3-5-b7 ascending. Ex.1-19B shows the octave displacements.

1-19A)                                                      1-19B)

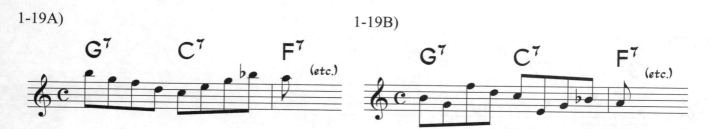

The "3rd to 5th" cycle is demonstrated in Ex.1-20. Ex.1-20A shows 3-5-b7-9 connecting to 5-3-1-b7. Ex.1-20B shows the octave displacements.

1-20A)                                                      1-20B)

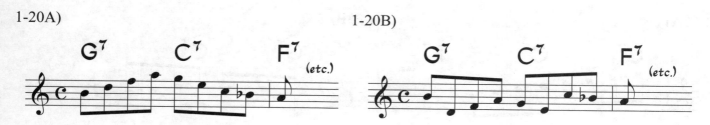

The ascending "3rd to 3rd" cycle, 3-5-1-b7, is shown in Ex.1-21A. We haven't yet looked at octave displacements for the 3rd-oriented patterns, so ex.1-21B shows the 3-5-1-b7 descending with displaced octaves. Ex.1-21C shows a one bar sequence alternating between the straight and octave-displaced patterns.

1-21A)                                                      1-21B)

1-21C)

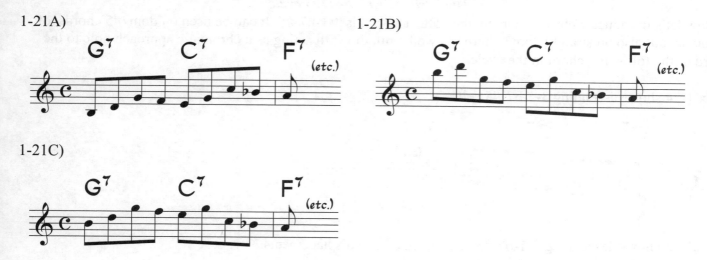

All the patterns we just examined use cells that are made up of all chord tones, or arpeggio permutations. If you recall, some of the cells from earlier in the chapter use descending scale lines. Let's analyze.

Ex.1-22A shows the descending 3rd-oriented pattern, 3-2-1-b7. Ex.1-22B shows 3-2-1-b7 ascending using octave displacements. Ex.1-22C (on the following page) shows a one bar sequence alternating between the straight and octave-displaced patterns.

1-22A)                                                      1-22B)

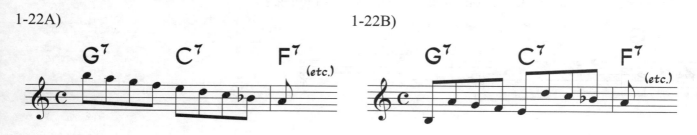

1-22C)

Ex.1-23A shows the descending 3rd-oriented pattern, 3-b9-1-b7. Ex.1-23B shows 3-b9-1-b7 ascending using octave displacements.

1-23A)                                          1-23B)

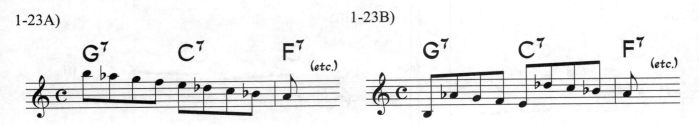

Incidentally, any one bar pattern using different or octave-displaced cells in the two halves of the measure can have the cells reversed. Try it and see. Note – if you reverse a "3rd to 5th" type pattern, or a "3rd to root" type pattern, the next measure must also be reversed.

### The "3rd to 3rd" dom7#5 cycle

Now let's introduce a chromatic note, the #5th. The cell is 3-1-b7-#5. It can be used on dom7#5 chords, of course, but also on straight dom7 chords as well, with the #5th acting as a chromatic approach note to the 3rd of the following chord in the cycle.

Ex.1-24 shows ascending 3-1-b7-#5 cells.

Ex.1-25 shows descending 3-1-b7-#5 cells using octave displacements.

Ex.1-26 shows a one bar sequence combining the last two examples.

*Using chromatics in the "3rd to 5th" cycle*

Next we'll add some chromatic notes to the "3rd to 5th" cycle. The first cell will be 3-b9-b7-7, with the natural 7th acting as a chromatic passing tone to the 5th of the following chord in the cycle. The second cell is still 5-3-1-b7. Being a "3rd to 5th" cycle, it automatically forms a one bar sequence.

Ex.1-27 shows a basic one bar sequence using the 3-b9-b7-7 cell followed by the 5-3-1-b7 cell.

Ex.1-28 shows the octave displacements for the one bar sequence using the 3-b9-b7-7 cell followed by the 5-3-1-b7 cell.

*Another very useful root-oriented triadic pattern*

The cells that follow contain only the root, 3rd, and 5th, the three notes of the basic triad. Four note cells are created by repeating one of the notes. The ascending triad cell is 1-3-5-3, while the descending cell is 1-5-3-5. Ex.1-29 shows the ascending cells.

Ex.1-30 shows the descending cells.

Ex.1-31 shows a combination forming a one bar sequence.

## A sample chorus on a jazz standard featuring extensive use of fast-moving dominant cycles

Keep in mind that any "root to root" cell can connect to any other "root to root" cell, or to the second half of any "3rd to root" pattern. Any "3rd to 3rd" cell can connect to any other "3rd to 3rd" cell, or to the first half of any "3rd to 5th" pattern. The halves can be swapped. Many variations are possible, and I can't

10

demonstrate them all, but I can show a hypothetical improvisation over one chorus of a well known jazz standard that almost all jazz musicians know (Ex.1-32). It's almost all material covered in this chapter, so you can do your own analysis. You can also improvise several more choruses of your own, using different cycle combinations each time.

# Quick II-V whole-step sequences

A II-V whole-step sequence is really a dominant cycle where the first chord of each pair has been changed into a mi7 chord, creating a chain of II-V progressions descending by whole-steps. This means it should be fairly easy to convert many, if not all, of the fast-moving dominant cycles we already know into "quick" (a shortened version of "fast-moving") II-V whole-step sequences by altering the first cell of each one bar sequence slightly so it fits the mi7 chord sound.

## "Root to root" patterns adapted to II-V whole-step sequences

*Root-oriented II-V whole-step sequences*
Ex.1-33 shows a "root to root" pattern forming a one bar sequence, a descending II-V whole-step sequence.

*Reversing the directions of the root-oriented cells*
The whole-step sequences we've done so far use an ascending 1-2-b3-5 cell on each II chord and a descending 1-b7-6-5 cell on each V chord. Now let's reverse the directions and use a descending 1-b7-6-5 cell on each II chord and an ascending 1-2-3-5 cell on each V chord. Since there is no b3rd in the II chord cells, the pattern can also be used for one bar sequences on fast-moving dominant cycles.

Ex.1-34 shows the reversed direction sequence.

(continued on next page)

12

*Triadic root-oriented II-V whole-step sequences*

Now let's look at "root to root" patterns using just the notes of the basic triads. We'll start by using an ascending 1-b3-5-b3 cell on each II chord and a descending 1-5-3-5 cell on each V chord.

Ex.1-35 shows the triadic root-oriented pattern.

*Reversing the directions of the triadic root-oriented II-V whole-step sequences*

The triadic patterns can also have the directions of their cells reversed, producing descending 1-5-b3-5 cells on the II chords and ascending 1-3-5-3 cells on the V chords.

Ex.1-36 shows the reversed triadic patterns.

(continued on following page)

## Combining the triadic and non-triadic cells

The triadic and non-triadic cells can be combined in four ways. I'm just going to show one bar of notes only for each combination. You'll want to work out all the usual exercises for each combination.

Ex.1-37 combines the ascending 1-2-b3-5 cell on the II chord with the descending triadic 1-5-3-5 cell on the V chord.

Ex.1-38 combines the descending 1-b7-6-5 cell on the II chord with the ascending triadic 1-3-5-3 cell on the V chord.

Ex.1-39 combines the ascending triadic 1-b3-5-b3 cell on the II chord with the descending 1-b7-6-5 cell on the V chord.

14

Ex.1-40 combines the descending triadic 1-5-b3-5 cell on the II chord with the ascending 1-2-3-5 cell on the V chord.

## "3rd to 3rd" patterns adapted to II-V whole-step sequences

By now you're ready to work out most of the specific exercises on your own. You can (and should) use the examples to work out fingerings for sequences that start high on your instrument and move down its full range.

*Scale-wise 3rd-oriented II-V whole-step sequences*

As I'm sure you recall, four-note cells that descend scale-wise in eighth-notes land on the same starting chord tone in the following chord in a fast-moving cycle, so a scale line descending from the 3rd in eighth-notes targets the 3rd of each following chord. By alternating with octave-displaced patterns we can form "3rd to 3rd" II-V whole-step one bar sequences.

Ex.1-41 shows a descending scale-wise II-V whole-step sequence. Each II chord cell is b3-2-1-b7, while each V chord cell is 3-2-1-b7 using octave-displacement.

Ex.1-42 shows another descending scale-wise II-V whole-step sequence, entire range, with the octave-displaced cells used on the II chords this time.

### Arpeggiated 3rd-oriented II-V whole-step sequences

All of the "3rd to 3rd" arpeggiated patterns consist of all chord tones and all use the b3-5-1-b7 cells going to the 3-5-1-b7 cells, either ascending or descending using octave displacements.

Ex.1-43 shows a II-V whole-step sequence using ascending cells on the II chords and descending octave-displaced cells on the V chords.

Ex.1-44 shows a II-V whole-step sequence using descending octave-displaced cells on the II chords and ascending cells on the V chords.

### Combining the scale-wise and arpeggiated cells

The scale-wise patterns and the arpeggiated patterns can be combined in various ways. These combinations will use the 3rd-oriented cells we already know, so again I'm just going to show one bar of notes only for each combination. You should work out all the usual exercises for each combination.

Ex.1-45 combines the descending b3-2-1-b7 cell on the II chord with the ascending 3-5-1-b7 cell on the V chord.

Ex.1-46 combines the ascending octave-displaced b3-2-1-b7 cell on the II chord with the descending octave-displaced 3-5-1-b7 cell on the V chord.

Ex.1-47 combines the ascending b3-5-1-b7 cell on the II chord with the descending 3-2-1-b7 cell on the V chord.

Ex.1-48 combines the descending octave-displaced b3-5-1-b7 cell on the II chord with the ascending octave-displaced 3-2-1-b7 cell on the V chord.

### 3rd-oriented II-V whole-step sequences using dom7b9 chords

The V chords in II-V whole-step sequences may be played as dom7b9 chords when using and combining scale-wise cells. Only one bar of notes only will be shown for each combination.

In ex.1-49 the II chord cell is b3-2-1-b7, while the V chord cell is 3-b9-1-b7 using octave-displacement.

Ex.1-50 shows the octave-displacement used on the II chord cell.

Ex.1-51 combines an arpeggiated II chord cell with a scale-wise dom7b9 V chord cell.

Ex.1-52 shows the same combination using octave-displacements.

See how many other combinations you can find. Many are possible using 3rd-oriented cells and mixing them up in many different ways.

18

# "3rd to 5th" patterns adapted to II-V whole-step sequences

"3rd to 5th" patterns can be adapted to II-V whole-step sequences in two different ways. First, each II chord can start on the 3rd with each V chord starting on the 5th, and second, the other way around (reversed) with each II chord starting on the 5th and each V chord starting on the 3rd.

*The basic "3rd to 5th" II-V whole-step patterns*
The basic patterns starting on the 3rd of the II chord will use ascending b3-5-b7-9 cells on the mi7 chords and descending 5-3-1-b7 cells on the dom7 chords.

Ex.1-53 shows the basic "3rd to 5th" pattern.

*The basic "3rd to 5th" reversed II-V whole-step patterns*
The basic patterns starting on the 5th of the II chord (reversed) will use descending 5-b3-1-b7 cells on the mi7 chords and ascending 3-5-b7-9 cells on the dom7 chords.

Ex.1-54 shows the reversed basic "3rd to 5th" pattern.

(continued on following page)

*The "3rd to 5th" II-V whole-step patterns using altered V chords*

Whole-step II-V sequences also sound good using altered V chords.

Ex.1-55 shows the "3rd to 5th" pattern using dom7#5 chords going down the entire range.

Ex.1-56 shows the "3rd to 5th" pattern using dom7#5b9 chords.

The "3rd to 5th" reversed II-V whole-step patterns using dom7b9 chords

Ex.1-57 shows the reversed "3rd to 5th" pattern using dom7b9 chords.

Ex.1-58 shows the reversed "3rd to 5th" pattern using dom7b9 chords with a chromatic passing tone.

The octave-displaced "3rd to 5th" II-V whole-step patterns

The "3rd to 5th" patterns can also use octave-displacement.

Ex.1-59 shows the basic "3rd to 5th" pattern using octave-displacement.

(continued on following page)

21

Ex.1-60 shows the octave-displaced reversed basic "3rd to 5th" pattern.

Ex.1-61 shows the octave-displaced reversed "3rd to 5th" pattern using dom7b9.

Ex.1-62 shows the octave-displaced reversed "3rd to 5th" pattern using dom7b9 chords with a chromatic passing tone.

22

# "3rd to root" patterns adapted to II-V whole-step sequences

"3rd to root" patterns can also be adapted to II-V whole-step sequences in two different ways. First, each II chord can start on the 3rd with each V chord starting on the root, and second, the other way around (reversed) with each II chord starting on the root and each V chord starting on the 3rd.

*The basic "3rd to root" II-V whole-step patterns*

The basic patterns starting on the 3rd of the II chord will use descending b3-1-b7-5 cells on the mi7 chords and ascending 1-3-5-b7 cells on the dom7 chords.

Ex.1-63 shows the basic "3rd to root" pattern going down the entire range.

*The basic "3rd to root" reversed II-V whole-step patterns*

The basic patterns starting on the root of the II chord (reversed) will use ascending 1-b3-5-b7 cells on the mi7 chords and descending 3-1-b7-5 cells on the dom7 chords.

Ex.1-64 shows the reversed basic "3rd to root" pattern.

*The octave-displaced "3rd to root" II-V whole-step patterns*

Ex.1-65 shows the basic "3rd to root" pattern using octave-displacement.

Ex.1-66 shows the octave-displaced reversed basic "3rd to root" pattern.

## Supplemental cells for fast-moving dominant cycles and II-V whole-step sequences

There are many other possible cells, especially ones using chromatics, that work well on fast-moving dominant cycles and on II-V whole-step sequences. I'm sure you've noticed that the II-V whole-step sequences are the same as dominant cycles but with the chord qualities alternating between mi7 and dom7. By now you should know how to work out all of the complete exercises once you get the notes for each pattern, so I'm just going to show one bar of notes only for each new sequence.

*Supplemental cells for "root to root" sequences*

Ex.1-67 shows a fast-moving dominant cycle using cells that approach each following chord root chromatically from above.

24

Ex.1-68 reverses the direction of the cells.

Ex.1-69 applies the same concept to a II-V whole-step sequence.

Ex.1-70 reverses the direction of the II-V cells.

In Ex.1-71 the first cell has no 3rd (the B natural is an off-the-beat passing tone) so it works for both dominant cycles and II-V sequences. Each following chord root is approached by a chromatic enclosure.

Ex.1-72 shows the octave-displaced version of the enclosure sequence.

*Supplemental cells for "3rd to 3rd" sequences*

Ex.1-73 shows a fast-moving dominant cycle using cells that approach each following chord 3rd with a chromatic enclosure.

Ex.1-74 reverses the direction of the cells.

In Ex.1-75, a II-V sequence, the 3rd of each dom7 chord is approached by a chromatic enclosure, while the 3rd of each mi7 chord is approached chromatically from above.

Ex.1-76 shows the octave-displaced version.

These supplemental cells can be combined with the other cells quite easily. Ex.1-77 shows the Gmi7 cell from 1-75 combined with a descending scale-wise dom7b9 cell on the C7.

Ex.1-78 combines an octave-displaced scale-wise cell on the Gmi7 with the C7 cell from 1-75.

*Some other supplemental sequences*

Ex.1-79 shows a "5th to 3rd" pattern using enclosures with double-chromatic approaches from below. The first cell has no 3rd so it works for both dominant cycles and II-V sequences.

Ex.1-80 shows a "root to 3rd" pattern using enclosures with double-chromatic approaches from below when approaching the second chord of each bar and double-chromatic approaches from above when approaching the first chord of each bar. Again, the first cell has no 3rd so it works for both dominant cycles and II-V sequences.

Ex.1-81 shows a variation combining the enclosures with double-chromatic approaches from below when approaching the second chord of each bar and a reversed enclosure with double-chromatic approaches from above when approaching the first chord of each bar. Once again, the first cell has no 3rd so it works for both dominant cycles and II-V sequences.

Ex.1-82 shows a "9th to 5th" II-V sequence featuring the "Gone But Not Forgotten-You're My Inspiration" quote (see *Line Games*, p.97).

Ex.1-83 shows a "9th to #root" II-V sequence. The "#root" is actually a chromatic lower-neighbor tone leading to the 9th of the C7.

Ex.1-84 shows a "9th to b7th" pattern. Even though the first chord cell has a B natural, it can still work on Gmi7 with the B forming part of a chromatic enclosure of the Bb, the 7th of C7.

Ex.1-85 shows a "b3rd to 13th" II-V sequence.

Ex.1-86 shows another "b3rd to 13th" II-V sequence.

Ex.1-87 shows an "11th to 13th" II-V sequence.

Ex.1-88 shows another "11th to 13th" II-V sequence.

Ex.1-89 shows a "5th to b7th" pattern. Again, even though the first chord cell has a B natural, it can still work on Gmi7 with the B forming part of a chromatic enclosure of the Bb, the 7th of C7.

Ex.1-90 shows a variation of the "5th to b7th" pattern.

28

Ex.1-91 is a variation of 1-90 with an octave-displacement.

Ex.1-92 shows another variation of the "5th to b7th" pattern.

Ex.1-93 is a variation of 1-92 using a descending chromatic cell on the Gmi7. Since the B natural is off-the-beat, I don't use it for dominant cycles. This same variation can be applied to 1-89 through 1-91.

Ex.1-94 shows a "13th to 13th" II-V sequence.

Ex.1-95 shows a "b7th to b7th" II-V sequence.

Ex.1-96 shows a "maj7th to 5th" II-V sequence.

Ex.1-97 shows a "#root to b7th" II-V sequence. The "#root" is actually a chromatic lower-neighbor tone leading to the 9th of the Gmi7.

## Chromatic II-V sequences

In addition to moving in whole-steps, II-V patterns also can descend chromatically by half-steps (for examples, check out "Stablemates," "Strollin'," "East Of The Sun," "I Can't Get Started," to name a few), and occasionally may even ascend by half-steps (for example, "Moment's Notice"). Most of the voice-leadings used for cycles and whole-step sequences are the same in the chromatic sequences, so many of the same patterns can be easily adapted. In general, alterations on the V chords don't translate well into the chromatic sequences, and occasionally a slight adjustment has to be made to to a V chord cell to keep the lines flowing.

*Basic root-oriented chromatic II-Vs*

Ex.1-98 demonstrates how to adapt a II-V whole-step sequence to create a a chromatic II-V sequence. It's based on the whole-step sequence shown in Ex.1-33, a basic root-oriented non-triadic pattern. You can use this example as a model to work out all the cell combinations for the chromatic II-V sequences, so again I'll show just one bar of notes only for each combination.

Ex.1-99 shows the reversed non-triadic pattern.

Ex.1-100 shows the basic root-oriented triadic pattern.

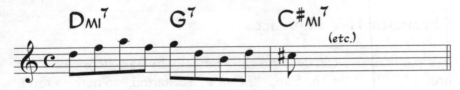

Ex.1-101 shows the reversed root-oriented triadic pattern.

Ex.1-102 shows a combination with the non-triadic pattern first.

Ex.1-103 shows the reversed combination with the non-triadic pattern first.

Ex.1-104 shows a combination with the triadic pattern first.

Ex.1-105 shows the reversed combination with the triadic pattern first.

*Basic 3rd-oriented chromatic II-Vs*

Ex.1-106 shows a basic 3rd-oriented scale-wise pattern with octave-displacement on the second cell.

Ex.1-107 shows a basic 3rd-oriented scale-wise pattern with the octave-displacement on the first cell.

Ex.1-108 shows a basic 3rd-oriented arpeggiated pattern with octave-displacement on the second cell.

Ex.1-109 shows a basic 3rd-oriented arpeggiated pattern with the octave-displacement on the first cell.

Ex.1-110 shows a combination with the scale-wise cell first and the arpeggiated cell second.

Ex.1-111 shows the octave-displaced version.

Ex.1-112 shows a combination with the arpeggiated cell first and the scale-wise cell second.

Ex.1-113 shows the octave-displaced version.

*Basic "3rd to 5th" chromatic II-Vs*

Ex.1-114 shows the basic "3rd to 5th" arpeggios with the II chord cells starting on the 3rd and the V chord cells starting on the 5th.

Ex.1-115 shows the octave-displaced version.

Ex.1-116 shows the basic "3rd to 5th" arpeggios with the II chord cells starting on the 5th and the V chord cells starting on the 3rd.

Ex.1-117 shows the octave-displaced version.

*Basic "3rd to root" chromatic II-Vs*

Ex.1-118 shows the basic "3rd to root" arpeggios with the II chord cells starting on the 3rd and the V chord cells starting on the root.

33

Ex.1-119 shows the octave-displaced version.

Ex.1-120 shows the basic "3rd to root" arpeggios with the II chord cells starting on the root and the V chord cells starting on the 3rd.

Ex.1-121 shows the octave-displaced version.

*Supplemental chromatic II-Vs starting on the root of each II chord*

Ex.1-122 shows a root-oriented sequence using a chromatic passing tone approaching the root of each V chord and a chromatic enclosure approaching the root of each II chord.

Ex.1-123 shows the octave-displaced version.

Ex.1-124 uses chromatic enclosures approaching both roots.

34

Ex.1-125 shows the octave-displaced version.

Ex.1-126 shows a "root to 3rd" sequence based on the old 5-to-3 device.

Ex.1-127 shows a variation.

Ex.1-128 shows another variation. The second cell descends scale-wise from the 3rd of the V chord.

Ex.1-129 is yet another variation. The second cell changes the order of the second cell's notes.

*Supplemental chromatic II-Vs starting on the 3rd of each II chord*

Ex.1-130 shows a 3rd-oriented sequence using the same V chord cell as 1-128.

Ex.1-131 shows a variation using the same V chord cell as 1-129.

Ex.1-132 shows a 3rd-oriented sequence using chromatic enclosures approaching both 3rds.

Ex.1-133 shows the octave-displaced version.

Ex.1-134 combines the first cell from 1-132 with the second cell from 1-128.

Ex.1-135 combines the first cell from 1-132 with the second cell from 1-129.

Ex.1-136 shows a "3rd to 5th" sequence using a chromatic approach tone.

Ex.1-137 shows a diatonic "3rd to 5th" sequence.

Ex.1-138 shows a variation using one chromatic note.

Ex.1-139 shows another variation using two chromatics this time.

Ex.1-140 is yet another variation using one chromatic.

Ex.1-141 shows a "3rd to 13th" sequence using a b3-b7-5-b3 cell on the II chords and a 13-5-#11-5 cell on the V chords.

Ex.1-142 is a "3rd to 13th" sequence using a b3-5-#4-5 cell on the II chords and the same V chord cell as used in 1-141.

### Supplemental chromatic II-Vs starting on the 5th of each II chord

Ex.1-143 shows a "5th to 7th" sequence. The II chord uses a 5-4-b4-2 cell. The b4th is not really a major 3rd, but functions as part of a chromatic enclosure approaching the b7th of the V chord. The V chord cell is the same as the II chord cell used in 1-142. Since these chromatic II-Vs use unaltered V chords, the cells used on the two different chords are often interchangeable. What was a b3-5-#4-5 cell on the II chord now becomes a b7-9-#1-9 cell on the V chord (the #root being a chromatic lower neighbor of the 9th).

Ex.1-144 shows another "5th to 7th" sequence using the 5-4-b4-2 cell on the II chords and a b7-9-13-5 cell on the V chords.

Ex.1-145 is the same as 1-144 but with an octave-displacement in the V chord cell.

Ex.1-146 shows a variation using a b7-#11-13-5 cell on the V chord.

Ex.1-147 shows another "5th to 7th" sequence using the same V chord cell as 1-146, but targets the 7th of the V chord with a chromatic line descending from the 5th of the II chord. The V chord could use any of the V chord cells starting on the b7th to form several more variations.

Ex.1-148 uses a 5-b7-9-11 arpeggio for the II chord cell.

Ex.1-149 is the same as 1-148 but with an octave-displacement in the II chord cell.

*Supplemental chromatic II-Vs starting on the 7th of each II chord*

Ex.1-150 is a "7th to 7th" sequence using a b7-9-11-b11 cell on the II chord and a b7-#11-13-5 cell on the V chord, but again the V chord could use any of the V chord cells starting on the b7th to form several more variations.

38

Ex.1-151 actually starts on the major 7th of the II chord. It's really part of a chromatic cell, 7-1-2-7, targeting the 5th of the V chord.

Ex.1-152 also starts on the major 7th of the II chord using a 7-2-b2-7 cell targeting the 5th of the V chord.

### Supplemental chromatic II-Vs starting on the 9th of each II chord

The first three examples demonstrating chromatic II-Vs starting on the 9th of each II chord use cell combinations cover in my earlier book, *Line Games*, in the section on bebop scales. Ex.1-153 uses the major 7th in the II chord cell.

Ex.1-154 uses chromatically descending major 2nds resulting in a chromatic enclosure of the 5th of the V chord.

Ex.1-155 uses the first five notes of the "Gone But Not Forgotten-You're My Inspiration" quote.

Ex.1-156 can be analyzed several different ways. I'll leave it up to you.

Ex.1-157 is a "9th to 7th" sequence. The 9-11-b11-9 cell can be followed by any of the V chord cells starting on the b7th to form several more variations.

The first cell in ex.1-158 is an often-used beginning for mi7 chords.

Ex.1-159 combines the "Cry Me A River" quote with a 13-5-#11-5 cell on the V chord.

Ex.1-160 combines a 9-b3-5-b7 cell on the II chord with a 13-5-#11-5 cell on the V chord.

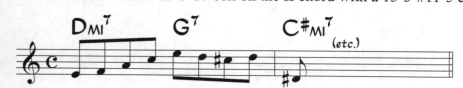

*Supplemental chromatic II-Vs starting on the #root of each II chord*
Patterns starting on the #root of each II chord are placed here because the #root not only replaces the 9th, it is a lower chromatic approach tone to the 9th. It starts a #1-2-4-b4 cell that is a double chromatic enclosure of the b7th of the V chord.

Ex.1-161 uses the #root cell followed by a "borrowed" b3-5-b7-9 II chord cell that becomes b7-9-11-13 of the V chord.

Ex.1-162 follows the #root cell with the same "borrowed" cell used in 1-143.

40

Supplemental chromatic II-Vs starting on the 11th of each II chord

Ex.1-163 combines the "Honeysuckle Rose" quote with a 13-5-#11-13 cell on the V chord.

Ex.1-164 uses a bebop scale type of line combined with the 13-5-#11-13 cell on the V chord.

Ex.1-165 shows an octave-displacement applied to the previous example.

Ex.1-166 shows another bebop style variation.

Ex.1-167 shows yet another variation.

Supplemental chromatic II-Vs starting on the 13th of each II chord

Ex.1-168 shows a "13th to 13th" sequence using a 13-b7-5-b3 cell on the II chord followed by a 13-5-#11-5 cell on the V chord.

Ex.1-169 shows another "13th to 13th" sequence using an ascending 13-1-b3-5 cell on the II chord followed by a 13-5-#11-5 cell on the V chord.

# Chapter 2 – Turnarounds

When jazz musicians use the term "turnaround," they are most often referring to a two-measure progression that occurs when the melody has reached a temporary resolution and has become inactive. It usually happens at the end of a section or of a chorus. Typically the two bars will have four chords lasting for two beats each so they are perfect for using the four-note cells. The progression is used to keep the harmony in motion and to target the first chord of the next section or chorus. The first chord of the next section or chorus may be a I chord or a II chord or a VI chord or sometimes a IV chord. The I chord is the most common, and once you know how to create turnarounds to the I chord the others should be easy.

## Standard turnarounds

The most commonly used turnarounds to the I chord are based on the famous I-VI-II-V-I progression. In the key of C major this would be Cmaj7-Ami7-Dmi7-G7 and back to C. This progression is entirely diatonic. Of course the chords could have some modifications and/or extensions and still be diatonic, for example C6/9-Ami11-Dmi9-G13. Since the turnaround happens when the melody is inactive, most jazz players will use some chromatic alterations and re-harmonizations during the turnaround to make things more interesting. Let's check out some actual recorded examples.

*Some actual examples of standard turnarounds*

Play Ex.2-1, from a recording of an improvised solo by Joe Pass.

It is a standard turnaround in the key of G major. In G the I-VI-II-V-I would be Gmaj7-Emi7-Ami7-D7-G. Notice that the first chord has two possible names, Gmaj7 or Bmi7. Joe's line will fit perfectly over either chord, although the recording definitely had a Bmi7, a III chord substituting for the I. The next chord, E7, is an alteration of the VI chord making it into a secondary dominant, the V of the II(V/II). This introduces a chromatic note, G#. The II chord is unaltered. The V chord is D7b9 using another chromatic, Eb.

Ex.2-2 is also from Joe Pass and uses a very similar harmonic scheme, but in the key of F major this time.

Notice that what Joe used in the second measure of the first example is used again in the first measure of this example. The V chord has two alterations, the #5 and the b9.

42

Ex.2-3 comes from Joe again, but in the key of Bb major.

The E natural in the first bar could be analyzed as the 13th of the G7, but really it's just part of a chromatic enclosure of the Eb in the next bar. The ascending chromatic scale cell on the V chord simply targets the final F note, the 5th of the I chord.

Ex.2-4 comes from a Wes Montgomery solo in the key of C major.

It has a similar harmonic scheme. Again, the line at the beginning will fit the I chord or the III chord, although the recording had the III chord. The VI again has been altered to make it a V/II. Wes plays two alterations on the A7, the b9 and the #5 (or b13). There are also two alterations on the G7, a #9 and a b9.

Ex.2-5 happens later in the same Wes solo. I'll leave the analysis up to you.

Ex.2-6, also in the key of C major, is from a Grant Green solo.

Ex.2-7 happens later in the same Grant Green solo.

Grant outlines a dom7b9 chord on the A7. The Eb on the Dmi7 is a chromatic approach tone to the 5th of the G7. The F on the final Cmaj7 is a diatonic lower neighbor resolving to the 5th.

Ex.2-8 comes from Pat Martino. It's in Bb major but continues to use the by now familiar harmonic scheme.

Ex.2-9 is from the same Pat Martino solo.

The G7 has a b9. The F# is a passing tone. The F7 has both a #9 and a b9. The final chord features the old 5-to-3 device, which we introduced in our previous Sher Music book, *Line Games*.

## Adapting II-V whole-step sequences to standard turnarounds

I'm sure you noticed that these examples closely resemble II-V whole-step sequences, especially when using the III-for-I substitute. The III in these turnarounds functions as a pivot chord. It's not only the III, it also functions as the II of the II since it's followed by the V of the II. Since this forms a II-V whole-step sequence, we should be able to easily adapt many of the II-V whole-step sequences we already know into standard turnarounds. Sometimes the adaptation will use some diatonic notes that will differ slightly from the pure whole-step pattern. For example, when using an Ami7 in the key of F you would probably use a Bb rather than the pure whole-step pattern's B natural.

### *Adapting scale-wise 3rd-oriented patterns to standard turnarounds*

First let's look at the old standard I-VI-II-V-I to demonstrate that we can use the voice-leading ideas we found in cycles and quick II-V sequences. The VI-II-V-I portion of the progression is all cycle-of-fifths movement (down in fifths and/or up in fourths), so we can go 3rd to 3rd easily by descending scale-wise in eighth-notes. To target the 3rd of the VI chord we descend from the 5th of the I chord. This note is also the 3rd of the III-for-I substitute chord.

Ex.2-10 demonstrates in the key of F major. Notice that it's really just the descending diatonic scale emphasizing the 3rd of each chord.

44

Ex.2-11 shows 2-10 adapted into a II-V whole-step sequenced used as a turnaround in F. Notice the Bb diatonic note on the first chord. The D7 has two chromatic notes, F# and Eb. This makes the entire first measure a descending G harmonic minor scale. The C7 has a b9, Db, making the second measure a descending F harmonic major scale.

Ex.2-12 shows the octave-displaced adaptation.

Ex.2-13 shows a sequential combination using the octave-displacement in the second half of each bar.

Ex.2-14 shows a sequential combination using the octave-displacement in the first half of each bar.

Many other combinations of straight and octave-displaced cells are possible. Your homework assignment is to find as many as you think you'll need.

*Creating more variations on the 3rd-oriented adaptations*
Now I'll show you some alternate cells you can use to form more variations.

Ex.2-15A can replace the first cell of 2-11 and 2-14. Ex.2-15B can replace the first cell of 2-12 and 2-13.

Ex.2-16 is a slight variation of 2-15 and is used the same way.

Ex.2-17 shows another variation in two different octaves, sill starting on the 5th of the I chord or the 3rd of the III-for-I substitute. Again, it's A for 2-11 and 2-14, B for 2-12 and 2-13.

Ex.2-18 shows a replacement cell for the first cell that starts on the 3rd of the I chord or the root of the III-for-I substitute. Again, it's A for 2-11 and 2-14, B for 2-12 and 2-13.

Ex.2-19 shows another variation starting on the 3rd of the I chord or the root of the III-for-I substitute and is used the same way.

Ex.2-20 is a cell that starts on the root of the I chord or the b6th of the III-for-I substitute. Again, it's A for 2-11 and 2-14, B for 2-12 and 2-13.

Ex.2-21 is something a little different. It shows a replacement cell for the first cell in the second measure. It changes the II chord from minor into a dominant, making it the V of the V. This is actually now an adaptation of a fast-moving dominant cycle into a standard turnaround. By using a dom7b9 it adds two new chromatic notes to our turnaround. 2-21A can replace the first cell of bar two of 2-11 and 2-13. 2-21B can replace the first cell of bar two of 2-12 and 2-14. Notice that the cell works on both G7b9 and on

Db7#11, its tritone substitution.

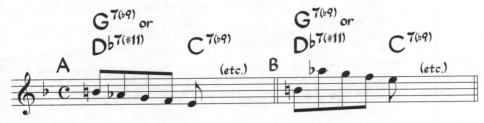

Most of the turnarounds that use the replacement cell from 2-21 will fit dominant cycles that actually start on A7alt, or its tritone substitute Eb7#11. For example, the original scale-wise cell, C-Bb-A-G is the #9-b9-1-b7 of A7alt and the 13-5-#11-3 of Eb7#11. However, the cell shown in 2-17 would be weak on A7 or Eb7, so Ex.2-22 shows an alternate for the adapted dominant cycle. It's spelled as b7-1-9-3 of Eb7, but can also represent 3-#11-#5-b7 of A7. Again, it's A for 2-11 and 2-14, B for 2-12 and 2-13.

*Adapting arpeggiated 3rd-oriented patterns to standard turnarounds*

The arpeggiated 3rd-oriented II-V whole-step sequences are especially easy to adapt to standard turnarounds.

Ex.2-23 shows an arpeggiated 3rd-oriented II-V whole-step sequence adapted to a standard turnaround. It's a chain of ascending cells.

Ex.2-24 shows the same thing using octave-displaced cells descending.

Ex.2-25 shows just one of many possible combinations of ascending cells and octave-displaced descending cells. See how many others you can find.

*Combining the scale-wise and arpeggiated patterns*

Ex.2-26 shows just one of many possible combinations of scale-wise and arpeggiated patterns. Experiment with creating other variations using this as a model. This will help you to develop fluency at improvising combinations that might be just right for some actual playing situation.

Ex.2-27 begins with a cell starting on the 3rd of the I chord or the root of the III-for-I substitution. It's 3-5-7-9 of the I chord or 1-b3-5-b7 of the III chord.

Ex.2-28 is all arpeggiated but uses a supplemental cell with a chromatic on the II chord.

Ex.2-29 combines the supplemental cells on the III and the II with scale-wise cells on the V/II and on the V chord.

*A turnaround using an adapted "5th to 3rd" sequence*
Ex.2-30 adapts a familiar "5th to 3rd" sequence to a stock turnaround.

*Turnarounds combining a variety of supplemental and standard cells*

Ex.2-31 adapts a "3rd to 3rd to 5th to 3rd to 5th" whole-step II-V sequence using some supplemental cells.

Ex.2-32 uses a similar concept, but starts on the root of the first mi7 cell and uses cells that resolve in different octaves.

Ex.2-33 uses a b3-5-b7-9 cell on the II chord followed by a #5-3-b9-b7 cell on the V chord.

Ex.2-34 shows the same thing but with octave-displacement on the II chord, moving the line into a lower register.

Ex.2-35 shows a variation on the II-V-I portion of the previous turnaround. The V chord cell has been changed to #5-3-1-b7.

Ex.2-36 shows another variation using #5-3-b9-7. The natural 7 is not harmonic, but just a chromatic leading-tone resolving to the 5th of the I chord.

Ex.2-37 is yet another variation. It has #5-3-1-b7 on the V chord but adds a note to the II chord cell, creating a five-note cell. A triplet is used to keep the line in time.

## Editing and phrasing the standard turnarounds

The last example brings up an interesting point: when improvising using four-note cells in eighth-notes, you don't have to play all in four-note cells or all in perpetual eighth-notes. You should experiment with using pick-up notes and should have the lines continue moving on the resolution chord. In other words, make phrases. You can also edit the lines by leaving notes out, and you can mix in some non-cellular melodies as well.

Ex.2-38 demonstrates.

It's based on 2-34 using the variation shown in 2-37. A three eighth-note pick-up was added in front. The chord is presumably F7, but it doesn't really matter because the pick-ups are targeting the first note of the original turnaround. Five notes are added at the end keeping the line moving past the point of resolution. The phrase starts and ends "off-the beat" to help keep things interesting.

Ex.2-39 is another variation.

No notes are added in front. Instead we use some "editing." A note is left out and the remaining notes are moved up, off-the-beats, creating rhythmic anticipation. Another note is added to the V chord cell, creating two triplets in a row for more rhythmic variety.

Ex.2-40 is based on 2-28 with three pick-ups added and, again, five notes added at the end.

Ex.2-41 also uses a three-note pick-up and mixes in a nice non-cellular melody on the II-V portion of the turnaround.

The II-V melody is based on the voice-leading created by the 9th on the II chord going to the b13th on the V chord and resolving to the 9th on the I chord. It ends with a "Honeysuckle Rose" quote.

Ex.2-42 uses the same II-V melody in a different turnaround, but only the turnaround itself is shown. You can supply your own pick-ups and/or edits and phrase ending.

*More supplemental turnarounds*

Ex.2-43 use an altered dominant cell from chapter one of my "Line Games" book.

Ex.2-44 introduces a new cell on the G7b9.

Ex.2-45 uses the new cell on the F7b9.

Ex.2-46 is a sequence using the new cell on both the G7b9 and the F7b9.

## Turnarounds using the #I diminished

Perhaps you've seen many turnarounds that start with the I chord going to the #I dim7 (or #Io7) before arriving at the II chord (the famous I-#Io-II-V turnaround). In the key of Bb it's Bbmaj7-Bo7-Cmi7-F7. You probably know that Bo7 is a substitute for G7b9. The 3rd, 5th, b7th, and b9th of G7 spell out a Bo7 chord. This means that it is still really a form of the standard turnaround. It also means that all the previous turnaround lines in Bb that used G7 or G7b9 can all be played over the Bbmaj7-Bo7-Cmi7-F7 turnaround. Thinking of the G7 as Bo7 may have its own implications, however, so let's check it out.

Ex.2-47 uses a triadic 1-3-5-1 cell on the I chord and a triadic 1-b3-b5-1 cell on the #I dim chord.

Ex.2-48 goes up the Bbmaj7 arpeggio, 1-3-5-7, then down the Bo7 arpeggio, bb7-b5-b3-1, before continuing with more familiar cells.

*Turnarounds using the #Io7 and the V7#5*

One interesting implication of the turnarounds using the #Io7 is the voice-leading from the roots of the first three chords to the #5th on the fourth chord, the V. In the key of Bb this is Bb on the I, B natural on the #Io, C on the II and C# on the V.

Ex.2-49 illustrates.

The middle two notes in each bar show the voice-leading. The first cell is 5-3-2-1 on Bbmaj7 followed by 1-b3-b5-bb7 on Bo7. The 1 in the first cell, Bb, moves directly to the 1 in the second cell, B natural. Next the third cell is 5-b3-2-1 on Cmi7 followed by #5-3-2-b2 with an octave-displacement on F7. The 1 of the Cmi7, C, moves directly to the #5, C#, of the F7#5.

Ex.2-50 shows another turnaround that has the same voice-leading line "hidden" inside.

The entire voice-leading line need not be present for the turnaround to be effective. Ex.2-51 has the Bb missing, but the B-C-C# is still powerful.

The ascending voice-leading line suggests further implications, as we'll see next.

## Turnarounds using the #II diminished

Now it's time to tackle the famous I-#Io-II-#IIo turnaround, which usually resolves to a III-for-I substitution or an inverted I with the 3rd in the bass (first-inversion). In Bb major this would be Bbmaj7-Bo7-Cmi7-C#o7 going to Dmi7 or Bb/D. Notice that the roots of the chords are the ascending voice-leading line. Let's try an example using what we already know.

Ex.2-52 starts the same as 2-47 but uses the 3-#5-2-b2 cell for F7#5 (as used in 2-50 and 2-51) as a b6-1-b5-4 cell for C#o7. Actually all the F7#5 cells in the previous section can be used on C#o7 as well.

Ex.2-53 starts with a descending 5-3-2-1 cell on the I chord followed by an ascending 1-b3-b5-bb7 cell on the #Io chord. This leads to a descending 5-b3-2-1 cell on the II chord followed by an ascending 1-b3-b5-bb7 cell on the #IIo chord. This last cell introduces the E natural note, which might not work so well on the F7#5 but is perfect for the C#o7.

### Substituting the A7 arpeggio for C#o7

As you recall, the Bo7 was a substitute for G7, so this suggests that the C#o7 may actually be a substitute for A7. Does this mean we can substitute an arpeggiated A7 cell for the C#o7? Let's find out.

Ex.2-54 shows a turnaround line that is literally arpeggios of Dmi7-G7-Cmi9-A7 used over the Bbmaj7-Bo7-Cmi7-C#o7. The diminished chords both use the "reverse" substitution and it sounds great.

Ex.2-55 uses triadic cells on the I-#Io-II portion and the A7 arpeggio on the #IIo.

Ex.2-56 uses all triadic cells starting on the 3rd of each chord. Notice that the diminished triads also spell out the upper portion of the "reverse" substitute dom7 chords.

Ex.2-57 shows the 3-5-1-b7 A7 cell that was used in 2-54 and 2-55. It can replace the F7#5 cell in 2-49, making it a I-#Io-II-#IIo turnaround. It can also replace the C#o7 cell in 2-53.

Ex.2-58 shows a variation, 3-1-5-b7, that can replace the last cell in all those examples (2-49, 2-53, 2-54, and 2-55).

Ex.2-59 shows a descending octave-displaced variation.

Ex.2-60 shows an A7 cell that starts on the root, 1-3-5-b7, and uses octave-displacement. This cell can replace the F7#5 cells in examples 2-50, 2-51, and 2-52, making them into I-#Io-II-#IIo turnarounds. You can also try using it to replace any kind of F7 cells starting on the 3rd that were used in earlier turnarounds.

## Turnarounds that use IV to #IV diminished

There are other kinds of turnarounds to the I chord that go to the IV chord instead of the II chord. They are common in the first two bars of the typical twelve-bar blues and in the fifth and sixth bars of Rhythm changes tunes (AABA tunes based on the changes to George Gershwin's "I've Got Rhythm"). One common version uses a #IVo7 chord to connect the IV back to the I.

*Some actual examples of turnarounds that use IV to #IV diminished*

Ex.2-61 is from a Joe Pass recording. Notice the use of our familiar 3-5-1-b7 A7 cell on the Eo7 chord. More on this later.

Ex.2-62, also from Joe Pass, shows a line over the same changes that uses a descending Eo7 arpeggio.

55

Ex.2-63, also from Joe, is literally a chain of arpeggios outlining Dmi7b5-G7-Cmi7-A7, but actually played over Bb9-Bb13b9-Eb6-Eo7. This shows a striking similarity to the previous turnarounds using the #IIo7. Indeed, they are often interchangeable.

Ex.2-64, again from Joe, shows another turnaround using the descending Eo7 arpeggio.

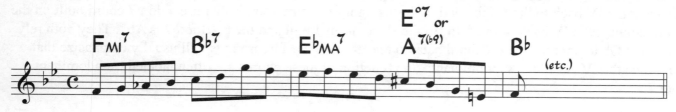

*Some supplemental turnarounds that use IV to #IV diminished*

Ex.2-65 uses the famous 3-5-1-b7 A7 cell on the Eo7.

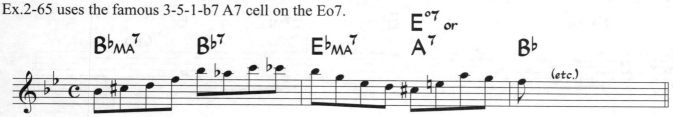

Ex.2-66 uses triadic cells on the Ebmaj7-Eo7.

Ex.2-67 uses the descending octave-displaced variation of the 3-1-5-b7 A7 cell on the Eo7.

Ex.2-68 uses the same cell an octave higher and uses a Bo7 arpeggio to imply Bb7b9.

56

Ex.2-69 uses a bebop scale passage in the first bar and triadic cells in the second bar.

## Turnarounds that use IV to IV minor

Another common variation on turnarounds that go to the IV chord instead of the II chord uses the IV minor to connect the IV back to the I. Included in this category are turnarounds that use a dom7 chord built on the bVII to connect the IV back to the I. In Bb the IV minor is Ebmi and the bVIIdom7 is Ab7. They both rely on the note Gb to connect the Eb chord back to the Bb, so these turnarounds will usually emphasize that note. Since the IV is called "subdominant", the function of these chords are often labeled "subdominant minor."

Ex.2-70 demonstrates with a turnaround that starts off the same as 2-66 but uses the IV minor instead of the #IV diminished.

Ex.2-71 follows an arpeggiated Fmi7-Bb7-Ebmaj9 with the same descending Eb minor triad used in the last example.

Ex.2-72 starts off the same as 2-67 but uses an Ebmi6 arpeggio instead of the A7 arpeggio, and also resolves to the 3rd of the I chord instead of the 5th.

Ex.2-73 shows the second bar of a turnaround using IV minor that can replace the second bar of 2-70 or 2-72. It employs a descending Ebmi-maj7 arpeggio resolving to the 3rd of the I chord.

Ex.2-74 is a variation that resolves to the 5th of the I chord. Again, it can replace the second bar of 2-70 or 2-72.

The subdominant minor chords are usually mi6 or mi-maj7 chords, but mi7 chords can be used as well. Ex.2-75 demonstrates with another variation of the second bar of 2-70 or 2-72.

Ex.2-76 starts with the same bebop idea used in 2-69 and finishes with a descending Ebmi-add9 arpeggio.

Ex.2-77 shows a turnaround starting with a bebop variation that targets the 3rd of the IV chord instead of the root, followed by triadic cells.

Ex.2-78 is a variation that changes the order of notes in the triadic cells.

Ex.2-79 shows one more IV minor turnaround before we move on. You should be able to create many more on your own.

Keep in mind that all of the Eb minor cells in these examples can be used with Ab7 chords replacing the Eb minor chords.

## Turnarounds that use an augmented sixth chord

You might be wondering what an augmented sixth chord is. They are not all that common in modern jazz, but occur frequently in ragtime and "trad jazz." They are usually misnamed as dom7 chords because the #6 sounds the same as the b7. The #6 occurs as the result of two voices moving in opposite directions (contrary motion) and can be clearly demonstrated using a progression that is very similar to the ones we've been doing that go to the IV chord. Let's investigate.

Ex.2-80 shows a guide tone line that implies the turnaround that uses the #IV diminished in the key of Bb. The half-note line goes Bb-D-Eb-E natural-F. Notice that it approaches the F with three consecutive chromatics from below. The line consists of the root of Bb, the 3rd of Bb7, the root of Eb, and the root of Eo7 going to the 5th of Bb.

Ex.2-81 shows a guide tone line that implies the turnaround that uses the IV minor in the key of Bb. This time the line approaches the F with three consecutive chromatics from above, forming the half-note line Bb-Ab-G-Gb-F. The line consists of the root of Bb, the b7th of Bb7, the 3rd of Eb, and the b3rd of Ebmi resolving to the 5th of Bb.

Ex.2-82 combines both lines into a composite that generates the augmented sixth. The line approaches the F from both above and below (in different octaves in this example). Because the lower line is descending it has a Gb, not F#, and because the upper line is ascending it has an E natural, not Fb. This creates the #6 interval, not a b7, so the chord is really Gb(#6). If you encounter it in a chart, it will likely be written as Gb7.

Ex.2-83 shows a turnaround based on the guide tone lines from 2-82.

Ex.2-84 is 2-77 with the last cell adapted to the Gb(#6).

Ex.2-85 shows it with a different adaptation.

Ex.2-86 is based on 2-72 converted to the #6 concept.

Ex.2-87 is based on 2-70 converted to the #6 concept.

Ex.2-88 is 2-66 converted to the #6 concept.

## Turnarounds that descend chromatically to the II chord

Now let's return to some turnarounds that use the II chord again instead of the IV chord. There are many turnarounds that approach the II chord from a half-step above (bIII). They may start on the III-for-I substitute, creating a descending chromatic bass line, or from the I chord.

*Turnarounds using bIII diminished going to the II chord*
Some turnarounds use a bIIIo7 going to the II chord (for example, bars 29 and 30 of "Out of Nowhere").

Ex.2-89 uses arpeggios of Dmi7-Dbo7-Cmi7 followed by a familiar F7b9 cell. The Dmi7 arpeggio is also a 3-5-7-9 cell for Bbmaj7.

Ex.2-90 uses arpeggios of Bbmaj7-Dbo7-Cmi7 followed by a familiar F7#5 cell. If the first chord was Dmi7 the Bbmaj7 arpeggio still works because the Dmi7 is a III-for-I substitute.

Ex.2-91 follows a 1-2-3-5 cell on the Bb chord with two triadic cells, Db diminished triad on the Dbo7 and an Eb major triad on the Cmi7. The Eb triad outlines the b3, 5, and b7 of the Cmi7. These are followed by a familiar F7b9 cell.

Ex.2-92 reveals an interesting fact. Bb6, Dbo7, and Cmi7 all have two notes in common, G and Bb. The other two notes descend chromatically, F and D on the Bb6 to Fb and Db on the Dbo7 to Eb and C on the Cmi7.

Ex.2-93 uses triadic cells on the first two chords followed by an octave-displaced b3-5-b7-9 arpeggio on the Cmi7 and a descending F7#5 arpeggio on the F7.

*Turnarounds using bIIImi7 going to the II chord*

Some turnarounds approach the II chord with a bIIImi7 chord. This usually implies starting on the III chord forming a pure chromatic descent. Sometimes, however, the bIIImi7 follows a I chord (for example, bars 29 and 30 of "You're My Everything").

Ex.2-94 alternates ascending and descending root-position mi7 arpeggios on the first three chords and finishes with the same familiar F7#5 cell used in 2-92.

Ex.2-95 reverses the directions of the alternation and also reverses the order of the first two notes of the F7#5 cell.

Ex.2-96 alternates b3-4-5-b7 cells with a b7-5-4-b3 (reversed) cell on the mi7 chords and uses the familiar F7b9 cell used in 2-91.

Ex.2-97 combines some familiar cells with one new one, 1-b3-5-4, on the Dbmi7.

### *Turnarounds using bIII7 going to the II chord*

The bIIIdom7 chord is actually a tritone substitution for the V of the II chord. In the following examples let's also use the tritone substitute Cb7 (bII7) instead of the regular V chord. This will create a descending chromatic bass line from III all the way down to I. Since these changes substitute for the standard turnaround changes, these lines are playable on the standard turnarounds as well.

Ex.2-98 is similar to 2-97, but the tritone substitutions use simple 1-2-3-5 cells.

62

Ex.2-99 also employs the 1-2-3-5 cells on the tritone subs, but use the b3-4-5-b7 cell on the Dmi7 and a 5-4-b3-1 cell on the Cmi7.

Since the III chord is a substitute for the I chord, all the last six examples can be used with a I chord replacing the first chord. We can also use I chord cells over either version of the turnarounds. Ex.2-100 uses the 1-2-3-5 cell on Bbmaj7 as the first chord. It also reverses the order of the first two notes on the Cb7 cell (2-1-3-5) for variety.

Ex.2-101 uses triadic cells on the first two chords and finishes the same as 2-100.

Sometimes turnarounds may use chromatic dominants all the way down from the bIII7 (for example, bars three and four of Monk's "Bemsha Swing"). Ex.2-102 starts with the same triadic cells as 2-101 and sequences them all the way through the turnaround.

Ex.2-103 is all 1-2-3-5 cells with a couple of permutations in the second bar.

Ex.2-104 uses all triadic cells.

Ex.2-105 starts with the same cell as 2-101, but now it's 5-6-7-9 of Bbmaj7.

Since the last four turnarounds use a IIdom7, *it* could have a tritone substitute. This could create a I-bIII7-bVI7-bII7 turnaround. Changing one or more of the dom7 chords into maj7 chords brings us to the classic "Dameron turnaround."

## The classic "Dameron turnaround"

The classic "Dameron turnaround" is named for the great jazz composer Tadd Dameron. He used it in his famous tune "Lady Bird." It can have several variations. If only one dom7 chord from the last paragraph is changed to maj7, it is almost always the bVI. The variations in Bb would be Bbmaj7-Db7-Gbmaj7-Cb7, Bbmaj7-Db7-Gbmaj7-Cbmaj7, and Bbmaj7-Dbmaj7-Gbmaj7-Cbmaj7. In the first variation the Cb7 could be replaced by an F7alt.

The second variation, I-bIII7-bVImaj7-bIImaj7, can be analyzed as a "phrygian" turnaround. It's an example of *modal interchange*. Since the Db7-Gbmaj7-Cbmaj7 are all diatonic in the key of Gb major, it means those three chords in the turnaround are functioning in the Bb phrygian mode. This chapter is about cellular improvisation so we're not going to employ that concept at this time, but it is something to think about.

If we use only triadic cells we can create lines which will work equally well on all the basic harmonic variations, so let's start there.

*Dameron turnarounds using only triadic cells*

Ex.2-106 shows a Dameron turnaround using triadic cells only.

Ex.2-107 shows another.

Ex.2-108 starts in a lower octave and works its way back up.

64

The starting notes of the first three cells descend in whole-steps in ex.2-109.

So far these examples have used cells that start on the root or 5th of each triad. These cells can be re-combined in many ways to create many more variations. Only the triadic chord names are given, but all the examples will fit all of the harmonic variations mentioned.

Ex.2-110 also has some triadic cells starting on the 3rd of the chord.

*Dameron turnarounds using only 1-2-3-5 cells*

The familiar 1-2-3-5 cells also have no 7ths. Therefore they also fit all of the Dameron turnaround variations.

Ex.2-111 is a turnaround using just the straight 1-2-3-5 cells on each chord.

In ex.2-112 the order of the first two notes in the first two cells is reversed for variety. This works on either or both of the first two chords because of the minor 3rd movement. Try all the combinations.

*Dameron turnarounds combining 1-2-3-5 cells (and permutations) with triadic cells*

Since both the 1-2-3-5 cells and the triadic cells have no 7ths, their combinations will also fit all of the Dameron turnaround variations.

Ex.2-113 begins with a reversed cell, 5-3-2-1, on the Bb chord and uses a triadic cell on the Cb chord.

Ex.2-114 also begins with the reversed cell and uses triadic cells on the Db and on the Cb chords.

### Combinations using another pentatonic cell

All of the triadic cells and the various 1-2-3-5 permutations are subsets of the major pentatonic scale (1-2-3-5-6-1). Since the pentatonic scale has no 7th, any cells derived from its notes will also fit all of the Dameron turnaround harmonic variations. Therefore we can easily add some new pentatonic cell variations into the combinations.

Ex.2-115 uses a 1-6-5-3 cell on the Cb chord.

Ex.2-116 uses the 1-6-5-3 cell on both the Db and the Cb chords.

### Dameron turnarounds using the Imaj7 chord

All of the harmonic variations on the Dameron turnarounds use a Imaj7 chord, so we can safely employ maj7 cells on the I chord in any Dameron turnaround.

Ex.2-117 uses a 5-6-7-9 cell on the Bbmaj7.

### Adding the bVImaj7 to the Dameron turnarounds

All of the harmonic variations on the Dameron turnarounds also use a bVImaj7 chord, so we can also safely employ maj7 cells on the bVI chord in any Dameron turnaround.

Ex.2-118 shows a combination using a 1-3-5-7 arpeggio on the Gbmaj7 chord.

Ex.2-119 also uses the same Gbmaj7 cell.

*An example using all maj7 chords*

Ex.2-120 fits the harmonic variation using all maj7 chords.

The first three chords all use the 1-3-5-7 cell, while the last cell is 13-5-#11-3, which will work on both Cbmaj7 and on Cb7 (and could also be #9-b9-1-b7 on F7alt). Since the 13-5-#11-3 cell is so flexible, try using it to replace the Cb cells in 2-118 and in 2-119.

*An example using the Bb minor pentatonic scale*

As you recall, the Dameron turnaround can be analyzed as a phrygian progression. Since the Bb minor pentatonic scale is a subset of the Bb phrygian mode, it can be used over the last three chords of a Dameron turnaround in Bb major.

Ex.2-121 follows a 3-5-7-9 cell on Bbmaj7 with a descending Bb minor pentatonic sequence that forms cells that will fit any of the harmonic variations of the Dameron turnaround.

*Dameron turnarounds using the bIIIdom7 chord*

Ex.2-122 uses an octave-displaced 1-3-5-b7 arpeggio to outline Db7.

Ex.2-123 is basically the same line starting an octave higher and using octave-displacement on the Gbmaj7 cell.

Ex.2-124 uses octave-displaced arpeggios on the first three chords and a 7-1-3-5 cell for the Cbmaj7.

Ex.2-125 re-introduces the old "5-to-3" device in Gb major to outline Db7 to Gbmaj7.

Ex.2-126 does the same with some octave-displacements and a permutation.

Ex.2-127 uses an enclosure to target the Db7 chord and chromatic passing tones to connect Db7 to Gbmaj7 and the Gbmaj7 to the Cb chord.

*Dameron turnarounds using the bIIdom7 chord or the V7alt chord*

Ex.2-128 starts with the same first three cells used in 2-124 and ends with a familiar melodic minor hexatonic scale cell, b7-9-13-5 on Cb7 (the A natural is used for the b7 to avoid Bbb and make it easier to read). The same cell could also represent 3-#5-#9-b9 on F7alt.

Ex.2-129 is the same as 2-128 but uses the familiar 3-b9-1-b7 cell on F7b9. The same cell could also represent b7-5-#11-3 on Cb7.

Actually, all the Cb cells used so far that don't have the major 7th could be used on both Cb7 chords and F7alt chords. I'll let you do your own analyses.

68

Ex.2-130A shows the b7-9-13-5 cell used on Cb7 in 2-128. It will usually resolve to the fifth of the I chord but can occasionally resolve to the 6th as well. It can replace the Cb cells in examples 2-107, 2-108, 2-110, 2-116, 2-117, and 2-126.

Ex.2-130B shows the same cell played an octave higher. It can replace the Cb cells in examples 2-106, 2-113, 2-115, 2-122, 2-123, and 2-125.

Ex.2-131A shows the 3-b9-1-b7 cell used on F7b9 in 2-129. It will almost always resolve to the 3rd of the I chord, but can occasionally resolve to the 5th or the #11th. It can replace the Cb cells in examples 2-107, 2-108, 2-110, 2-116, 2-117, and 2-126.

Ex.2-131B shows the 3-b9-1-b7 cell played an octave higher. It can replace the Cb cells in examples 2-106, 2-113, 2-115, 2-122, 2-123, and 2-125.

*Dameron turnarounds using "hidden" descending whole-step sequences*
One interesting feature of Dameron turnarounds is the possibility of discovering "hidden" sequences that descend by whole-steps. Play ex.2-132.

It's really just a sequence of triadic cells descending by whole-steps, but the major triads are F, Eb, Db, and Cb before resolving to Bb. How does it work? Well, the F triad is the 5th, 7th, and 9th of the Bbmaj7. The Eb triad is the 9th, #11th, and 13th of either Db7 or Dbmaj7. The Db triad is the 5th, 7th, and 9th of the Gbmaj7 while the Cb triad is, of course, the root, 3rd, and 5th of either Cb7 or Cbmaj7.

Ex.2-133 uses the same triads but uses a combination of cells that hide the obvious whole-step descent.

Ex.2-134 again employs the same triads but uses a combination of cells that actually climbs as the triads "descend." (See following page.)

Sometimes a descending whole-step sequence can have a slight modification to make it fit a specific harmonic variation. Ex.2-135 uses fourth chords descending by whole-steps. The second cell is modified with a Cb note, making the bottom fourth into an augmented fourth. This allows the sequence to be used on the harmonic variation using the Db7 chord. The first cell is 9-3-6-9 of Bbmaj7. The second cell is 13-b7-3-13 of Db7. The third cell is another 9-3-6-9 on Gbmaj7. The last cell is 5-6-9-5 of either Cb7 or Cbmaj7.

Ex.2-136 shows another set of fourth chords descending by whole-steps. This time no modification is required because none of the cells contain any kind of 7th in relation to the underlying chords. The first cell is 5-6-9-5 of Bb. The second cell is 9-3-6-9 of Db. The third cell is another 5-6-9-5 on Gb. The fourth cell is 1-9-5-1 on Cb.

The next two examples will show sequences using the inversions of the fourth chords from 2-136.

Ex.2-137 uses the "first inversion" of the quartal triad cells used in 2-136.

Ex.2-138 uses the "second inversion" of the quartal triad cells used in 2-136.

Discovering these hidden whole-step sequences reminds me of a type of turnaround that actually does descend by whole-steps, the "C.T.A." turnaround.

# The "C.T.A." turnaround

The "C.T.A." turnaround gets its name from the Jimmy Heath tune "C.T.A.", a variation on rhythm changes that uses a turnaround using descending whole-step changes in bars 1-2 and in bars 3-4 of the A sections. The changes in Bb (the usual key, by the way) are Bb7, Ab7, Gb7, F7. Sometimes the tritone substitution for F7, Cb7, is used.

The "C.T.A." changes are originally all dom7 chords, but we can use triadic and other kinds of cells as well.

Ex.2-139 shows a simple triadic C.T.A. turnaround sequence.

Ex.2-140 shows a non-sequential triadic C.T.A. turnaround.

Ex.2-141 combines 1-2-3-5 permutations on the Bb and Gb chords with a triadic cell on the Ab chord and an arpeggiated F7 cell on the F7 chord.

Ex.2-142 starts with a triadic cell followed by two 1-2-3-5 permutations and finishing with the F7 cell.

Ex.2-143 begins with a 1-2-3-1 cell followed by two triadic cells and finally the same F7 cell.

Ex.2-144 is similar to 2-143 but uses a Cb triadic cell as a tritone substitution for F7.

Ex.2-145 is all triadic cells and again uses a Cb triadic cell.

That should be enough to enable you to create as many C.T.A. variations as you want. Now I'd like to touch briefly on Coltrane's "Giant Steps" changes. It's not really a turnaround, but it is very similar to Dameron turnarounds, so this would be the time to take a look.

## Coltrane's "Giant Steps" changes

The Dameron turnaround in Bb could be Bbmaj7-Db7-Gbmaj7-F7 going back to Bb. If we transpose it up a half-step we get Bmaj7-D7-Gmaj7-F#7 going back to B. Notice that the first root movement (B to D) is up a minor third. Coltrane repeats this motion by going up a minor third from the Gmaj7 to a Bb7, which then resolves to Ebmaj7. This results in the changes Bmaj7-D7-Gmaj7-Bb7 going to Ebmaj7, the first three bars of "Giant Steps". That's all we're going to look at here because once you get through the first three bars you can solve the whole tune. For more complete versions you can check out excellent chapters on Coltrane's changes in *The Serious Jazz Book II – The Harmonic Approach* by Barry Finnerty, *The Jazz Musician's Guide to Creative Practicing* by David Berkman, and *The Jazz Theory Book* by Mark Levine (all available from Sher Music Co.).

*Coltrane changes using cells without 7ths*

All the changes in the first three bars of "Giant Steps" have major thirds so once again triadic cells and other cells without 7ths will work fine. For now the chord symbols will be triadic (the lines still work on the 7th chords, however). It's in three different keys so there will be no key signatures.

Ex.2-146 is similar to the Dameron turnaround shown in 2-108, but transposed and converted into Coltrane changes. It uses all triadic cells.

Ex.2-147 is roughly similar to to the Dameron turnaround shown in 2-109 transposed and converted into Coltrane changes. Again it uses all triadic cells.

72

Ex.2-148 is similar to the Dameron turnaround shown in 2-114 transposed and converted into Coltrane changes. It uses a mixture of triadic cells and 1-2-3-5 permutations.

Ex.2-149 also uses a mixture of triadic cells and 1-2-3-5 permutations. It starts off similar to the Dameron turnaround shown in 2-119.

Ex.2-150 alternates between triadic cells and 1-2-3-1 cells.

Ex.2-151 shows the reverse alternation.

*Coltrane changes using cells with 7ths*

Ex.2-152 is based on 2-124 transposed and converted into Coltrane changes using cells that contain the 7ths of the chords.

Ex.2-153 has the same notes as 2-152 but uses some octave-displacements to re-shape the line.

73

Ex.2-154 is based on 2-126 transposed and converted into Coltrane changes, also using cells that contain the 7ths of the chords.

Ex.2-155 has the same notes as 2-154 but uses some octave-displacements to re-shape the line.

Ex.2-156 shows another combination using all familiar cells.

Ex.2-157 shows yet another combination using all familiar cells.

### Coltrane changes using "hidden" descending whole-step sequences

Since the Coltrane changes are closely related to the Dameron turnarounds and the Dameron turnarounds contain hidden descending whole-step sequences, we can find hidden whole-step sequences in the Coltrane changes as well.

Ex.2-158 is based on 2-135 transposed and converted into Coltrane changes. The second and fourth cells are modified to fit the dom7 chord qualities.

Ex.2-159 is based on 2-136 transposed and converted into Coltrane changes.

Ex.2-160 is based on 2-137 transposed and converted into Coltrane changes.

Ex.2-161 is based on 2-138 transposed and converted into Coltrane changes.

I know there are many other cells and cellular combinations for Coltrane changes, but I think we've seen enough to get the idea of how to do it, so I think it's time to move on.

# Chapter 3 — Longer II-V Progressions

*Using four-note cells on slower-moving changes*

Four-note cells are perfect for fast-moving changes (two beats per chord), but they are also useful for slower-moving changes as well. In this chapter we'll see how to string four-note cells together into longer lines for II-V progressions with four beats per chord.

*Introduction to using four-note cells on II-V progressions with four beats per chord*

Let's start by looking at some cellular combinations using only some familiar cells from chapter 1. We are going to start by playing some unaltered II-V progressions. As you recall, the chromatic II-V sequences always used unaltered V chords, so we'll use cells from examples 1-98 through 1-169. We'll stay in the key of C for the examples, using Dmi7 to G7.

## Unaltered long II-V changes

Play Ex.3-1.

The first measure uses the cell combination from Ex.1-98. The second measure uses the cell combination from Ex.1-152. Notice that both measures were originally designed for Dmi7 to G7 lasting only two beats each. Since the V chord is unaltered we can treat the II-V as one sound, so the lines work on just Dmi7, or just G7, or just G7sus, or Dmi7-G7 (two beats each) repeated in the second bar (as in Duke's "Satin Doll"), or on Dmi7 in the first bar and G7 in the second. The next note if this line were to continue would most likely be G. It could on occasion be an Ab as part of a chromatic enclosure of G. The G works if the II-V is resolving to I and also works if it's modal and we're continuing with the Dmi7-G7 sound.

Now play Ex.3-2.

The first cell is the same as the first cell in ex.1-120. The second cell is the same as the second cell from Ex.1-131. The next two cells are the same combination used in Ex.1-156. If the II-V resolves to I the next note in the line could be B, the major 7th of Cmaj7, or the G below the G#, the 5th of Cmaj7. In a modal situation there are other good choices including C or C#.

*A few supplemental cells*

Because the lines stay on the II-V longer than they do in the chromatic II-V sequences it will be useful to have a few supplemental cells that will assist us for this purpose.

Ex.3-3 is a simple ascending scale fragment from the root of Dmi7 or the 5th of G7. The most likely next note would be A if the Dmi7-G7 sound is continuing. It might be E, especially if it's resolving to Cmaj7.

Ex.3-4 uses three notes with a repeated A to form a four-note cell. G is the most likely next note.

Ex.3-5 also starts on A but doesn't repeat any notes. The next note could be almost anything, but if the Dmi7-G7 sound is continuing two of my own favorites would be C# and G.

Ex.3-6 has a chromatic (Eb) at the end that practically makes the D shown in parenthesis the only possible choice for the next note. The only other possibility that comes to mind is a C# appoggiatura to the D.

Ex.3-7 also starts on A and seems to target the note E.

Ex.3-8 starts on the 9th of Dmi7 (the 13th of G7) and is most likely going to the 3rd of Dmi7 (the 7th of G7) shown in parenthesis.

Ex.3-9 also starts on the 9th of Dmi7 (the 13th of G7) and is most likely going to the 3rd of Dmi7 (the 7th of G7) shown in parenthesis.

Ex.3-10 starts on the b3rd of Dmi7 (the 7th of G7) and the Eb has the same implications as it did in Ex.3-6.

You may also recognize many of the cells used in this chapter as being familiar from the first three chapters of my previous book, *Line Games* (Sher Music Co.).

77

Of course examples 3-1 and 3-2 are both unaltered long II-V combinations starting on the root of the II chord, so we've already begun. These long II-V combinations can be resolved to their I chords. They can also continue as modal lines and they can also be practiced as descending and ascending whole-step and half-step sequences.

The chord symbols for the following examples will read Dmi7 for the first measure and G7 for the second measure, but keep in mind that all the examples could be Dmi7 for two beats and G7 for two beats in the first bar and the same repeated in the second bar, or Dmi7 for the whole two measures, G7 for the whole two measures, or G7sus for the whole two measures.

Ex.3-11 starts with the scale fragment cell shown in 3-3 (played down an octave) and follows it with the cell shown in 3-4. Next comes the cell combination shown in Ex.1-167 (also played down an octave). The most likely next note for the line to resolve to the I chord would be G. The most likely next note for the line to continue might be C#.

This whole example can and should be played up an octave too. Also don't neglect transposing into all other keys. Of course that goes for all the examples.

Ex.3-12 also starts with the cell from 3-3 but follows it with the cell shown in 3-5. The second bar uses the combination shown in ex.1-152. The most likely next note for the line to resolve to the I chord or to continue would be G.

Ex.3-13 again starts with the cell from 3-3 but this time follows it with a cell shown in Ex.1-148. Next comes the cell combination shown in Ex.1-140. The most likely next note for the line to resolve to the I chord or to continue would be G.

Ex.3-14 uses the the scale fragment in the higher octave and follows it with the cell shown in 3-7 (also played up an octave). The second bar uses the combination shown in Ex.1-154. The most likely next note for the line to resolve to the I chord or to continue would be G (or an Ab as part of a chromatic enclosure of G).

78

Ex.3-15 starts the same as 3-14 but the second cell comes from Ex.1-147. This is followed by the combination shown in Ex.1-138. Again the most likely next note is G.

Up until now when we've used combinations of two cells they've been fit neatly into a measure, but actually the combinations can easily cross the bar lines as well. Ex.3-16 starts with the same first cell as 3-1 and then uses the combination shown in Ex.1-150 for the next two cells, the last cell in the first measure and the first cell of the second measure. The last cell is the first cell from Ex.1-130 reversed. It actually comes from chapter 1. The most likely next note would be E.

Like Ex.3-2, Ex.3-17 starts with the first cell from Ex.1-120 followed by the second cell from Ex.1-131. The second bar uses the combination shown in Ex.1-153. Next note, probably G.

Ex.3-18 also starts with the ascending Dmi7 arpeggio, but an octave lower this time. The second cell is the same as the first cell from Ex.1-155. The second measure uses the combination shown in Ex.1-129. The most likely next note would be E.

Ex.3-19 starts with the same cell followed by the first cell from Ex.1-157. The second measure uses the combination shown in Ex.1-140, likely followed by G.

Ex.3-20 starts with the combination from Ex.1-129 (played up an octave) followed by the combination shown in 1-156. If the line resolves to I the next note could be B or the G below the G#. If it continues modally the next note could also be a C#. (See following page.)

Ex.3-21 also starts with the combination from Ex.1-129 followed by the combination shown in 1-154.

Ex.3-22 starts with a descending scale fragment that's actually from the second chapter. The next two cells are the combination shown in Ex.1-165, crossing the bar line this time, and finishing with our familiar G-targeting cell.

*Unaltered long II-V combinations starting on the b3rd of the II chord*
Ex.3-23 starts on the b3rd of the II chord with a cell combination borrowed from Ex.1-130. This is followed by the combination shown in 1-154 targeting the G note.

Ex.3-24 also starts on the b3rd of the II chord using the cell combination shown in 1-131 followed by the combination shown in 1-153, also targeting the G note.

Ex.3-25 starts with the same cell played an octave lower. Next is the first cell from Ex.1-152 played in the second half of the bar, followed by the combination shown in 1-129 and probably going to the note E.

80

Ex.3-26 begins by using the cell combination shown in 1-137 and follows it with the cell combination borrowed from Ex.1-165. The most likely next note is D.

Ex.3-27 starts with the same first measure with the second measure using the combination shown in 1-167. My favorite next note is G.

Ex.3-28 also starts with the same first measure. The second measure uses the combination from 1-163. My favorite next note is G.

Ex.3-29 has the same notes as 3-28 but uses an octave-displacement in the second bar.

Since the last four examples all began with the same cell, we can multiply the combinations by coming up with some variations on that first cell. Practice starting all of the last four examples with each of the next three variation cells.

Ex.3-30 shows the first cell borrowed from 1-138.

Ex.3-31 shows the first cell borrowed from 1-139.

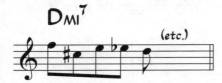

81

Ex.3-32 shows the first cell borrowed from 1-140.

*Unaltered long II-V combinations starting on the 5th of the II chord*

Play Ex.3-33. The first cell comes from 3-5. I'm not going to give sources for the remaining cells in the example because they're some of the same ones we've been using and I'm sure you know them well by now.

Ex.3-34 starts with the cell shown in 3-6. You know the rest.

Ex.3-35 begins with the combination shown in 1-148.

Ex.3-36 is a different combination starting with the same cell as 3-35.

Ex.3-37 begins with the cell shown in 3-7. The last cell we haven't seen for a while. It comes from Ex.1-116. The most probable next note is G.

82

Ex.3-38 shows another combination that starts with the same cell as 3-37.

Ex.3-39 starts with the second cell from 1-167 (same as the last cell in 3-38).

Ex.3-40 starts with the first cell from examples 1-143 through 1-146. Notice that the second cell is from 3-32, a variation. Try replacing it with the cells shown in 3-31, 3-30, and the first cell in 3-29 to multiply the possibilities.

Ex.3-41 starts with the combination shown in 1-144. Try starting with the combinations from 1-145 and 1-146 for more variations.

Ex.3-42 replaces the first cell of 3-40 with the first cell from 1-147. Try starting all of the combinations going back to 3-40 with this cell for even more possibilities.

Ex.3-43 begins with the combination shown in 1-143. Also try it replacing the first cell with the first cell from 3-42.

*Unaltered long II-V combinations starting on the b7th of the II chord*

In Ex.3-44, which starts on the b7th of the II chord, the first two cells come from the combination shown in 1-150.

Ex.3-45 begins with the same first cell but continues with a different combination.

Ex.3-46 uses the cell played an octave lower.

Ex.3-47 shows another combination starting with the same cell.

The first cell in Ex.3-48 can be thought of in two different ways. It can be the cell from 3-7 with the first two notes reversed or it can be the first cell from 1-131 with the entire cell reversed.

Ex.3-49 reverses the entire first cell from 3-2.

*Unaltered long II-V combinations starting on the maj7th of the II chord*

The II chord is a mi7 chord with a b7th, but the maj7th can be a colorful chromatic neighbor-tone that can be a great starting note for II-V lines.

84

Ex.3-50 starts with the combination shown in 1-151.

Ex.3-51 begins with the same first cell, then continues with a different combination.

Ex.3-52 also starts with the combination shown in 1-151 and follows it with the combination from 1-163 played down an octave.

Ex.3-53 is the same as 3-50 but begins with the combination shown in 1-152. The second cell is the same, so the first cell can replace the first cell of any example going back to 3-51.

Ex.3-54 starts with the first cell from 1-151 played an octave lower.

Ex3-55 starts with the first cell from 1-152 played an octave lower.

*Unaltered long II-V combinations starting on the 9th of the II chord*

Ex.3-56 is a line beginning with the combination shown in 1-153.

85

Ex.3-57 shows a cell borrowed from 1-232 that can replace the first cell in 3-56 for variety.

Ex.3-58 shows a cell borrowed from 1-233 that also can replace the first cell in 3-56.

Ex.3-59 starts with the combination from 1-156.

Ex.3-60 begins with the same first cell as 1-157 but continues with a different combination.

Ex.3-61 starts with the combination from 1-158.

Ex.3-62 starts with the combination from 1-159.

Ex.3-63 begins with the same first cell as 1-160 but continues with a different combination.

*Unaltered long II-V combinations starting on the 11th of the II chord*

Ex.3-64 starts with the combination shown in 1-163.

The first cell in 3-64 can be replaced with the first cell from 1-164. It could also be replaced with the first cell from 1-166.

Ex.3-65 starts with the combination shown in 1-165.

Ex.3-66 starts with the combination shown in 1-167.

*Unaltered long II-V combinations starting on the 13th of the II chord*

The first cell in Ex.3-67 comes from 1-168.

The first cell in Ex.3-68 comes from 1-169 and is followed by an interesting cell that appears at the start of 1-161 and 1-162.

*Unaltered long II-V combinations starting on the #root of the II chord*

The #root is part of a double chromatic enclosure of the mi3rd of the II chord (or the b7th of the V chord).

Ex.3-69 starts with the interesting cell that was used in the second half of the first bar of 3-68. The second cell is the same as the first cell in 3-29, so it can be replaced with any of the cells shown in 3-30, 3-31, and 3-32 for more variations. (See following page.)

Ex.3-70 shows another combination starting with the #root cell.

Ex.3-71 shows yet another.

## Long II-V changes using tritone substitution

*Using tritone substitution to create altered dominant sounds*

In chapters 1 and 2 of *Line Games*, altered dominant sounds were created using melodic minor hexatonic scales and bebop melodic minor scales and altered arpeggios. Using the cellular concept altered dominant sounds can be created with the same cells used in the unaltered II-V examples by using tritone substitution. If cell combinations from the "key" that's a tritone away from the key of the basic II-V are "superimposed" over the V chord altered dominant sounds are implied. In the cellular approach we can "re-think" Dmi7 to G7alt, four beats each, as Dmi7 to G7(unaltered) to Abmi7 to Db7(unaltered), two beats each. Dmi7-G7 is the II-V in the key of C major, while Abmi7-Db7 is the II-V in the key of Gb major, a tritone away from C.

*Some actual examples using tritone substitution*

Play Ex.3-72.

This comes from a Wes Montgomery solo. It happens in the fourth bar of a blues in F over the F7 chord going to the Bb7 chord in the next bar. The line clearly implies F#mi7-B7 going to the Bb7. It does not really come from an F altered scale. Notice the E natural note. It's very dissonant on F7 but makes perfect sense when seen (or, more importantly, heard) as the b7th of F#mi7 going to the 3rd of B7. John Coltrane definitely used this concept and he was one of Wes' major influences.

Now play Ex.3-73.

This also comes from a Wes Montgomery solo. It's the third and fourth bars of a blues in D, again over a dominant I chord, D7, which will go to a G7 in the next (fifth) bar. The tempo of this blues is much slower, giving Wes more time to fill the measures with longer ideas. Wes plays a line in the first measure of the example that clearly sounds like Ami7. In the next measure he plays a line that actually mimics the previous measure somewhat, but a tritone away, sounding like Ebmi7.

Sometimes this concept may be written into a tune. Bill Evans wrote a tune based on Rhythm changes that replaces D7-G7-C7-F7, two bars each, with Ami7-D7-Ebmi7-Ab7-Dmi7-G7-Abmi7-Db7-Gmi7-C7-Dbmi7-Gb7-Cmi7-F7-F#mi7-B7, only two *beats* each.

The second Wes example above (3-73) implies that sometimes a cell combination can be literally replicated a tritone away. Let's start by looking at some of those since they convey the tritone substitution concept so clearly.

*Long II-V changes using literal tritone replication*

Play Ex.3-74.

It starts on the root of the II chord with the combination used in the first bar of 3-11, then continues from the root of Abmi7, replicating the entire combination a tritone away. Since tritone substitution implies an altered V chord, the next chord will most likely be the I chord, so I'm showing a probable next note for the line to continue. In this case the note is E, but whenever the E immediately follows an Eb, a D note is a possible alternate choice.

*Long II-V literal tritone replications starting on the root of the II chord*

Ex.3-75 uses some familiar cells and replication up a tritone.

Even though the chord symbols read Dmi7 for one bar and G7alt for one bar, the cells clearly outline Dmi7-G7-Abmi7-Db7, two beats each.

The tritone is the only symmetrical interval. This means up a tritone and down a tritone is the same distance, so depending on the cell combination used it may be better to to replicate down a tritone rather than up.

Ex.3-76 also starts on the root of the II chord and uses some familiar cells with replication down a tritone.

*Long II-V literal tritone replications starting on the b3rd of the II chord*
Ex.3-77 starts on the b3rd of the II chord and uses replication up a tritone.

Ex.3-78 also starts on the b3rd of the II chord and uses replication down a tritone.

Notice that the first cell is the same as the first cell from 3-29, so it can be replaced with any of the cells shown in 3-30, 3-31, and 3-32 for more variations.

*Long II-V literal tritone replications starting on the 5th of the II chord*
Ex.3-79 starts on the 5th of the II chord and uses replication up a tritone.

Ex.3-80 also starts on the 5th of the II chord and uses replication down a tritone.

*Long II-V literal tritone replications starting on the b7th of the II chord*
Ex.3-81 starts on the b7th of the II chord and uses replication up a tritone.

90

Ex.3-82 also starts on the b7th of the II chord and uses replication down a tritone.

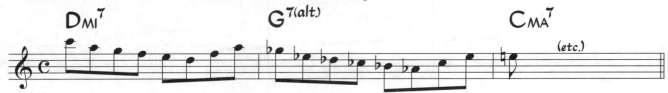

*Long II-V literal tritone replications starting on the maj7th of the II chord*

Ex.3-83 starts on the maj7th of the II chord and uses replication up a tritone.

Ex.3-84 also starts on the maj7th of the II chord and uses replication down a tritone.

*Long II-V literal tritone replications starting on the 9th of the II chord*

Ex.3-85 starts on the 9th of the II chord and uses replication up a tritone.

Ex.3-86 also starts on the 9th of the II chord and uses replication down a tritone.

Notice that the first cell is the same as the cell shown in 3-57, a variation, so it can be replaced with the cell shown in 3-58 or with the first cell from 3-56 for more variety.

*Long II-V literal tritone replications starting on the 11th of the II chord*

Ex.3-87 starts on the 11th of the II chord and uses replication up a tritone.

Ex.3-88 also starts on the 11th of the II chord and uses replication down a tritone.

*Long II-V literal tritone replications starting on the 13th of the II chord*

Ex.3-89 starts on the 13th of the II chord and uses replication up a tritone.

Ex.3-90 also starts on the 13th of the II chord and uses replication down a tritone.

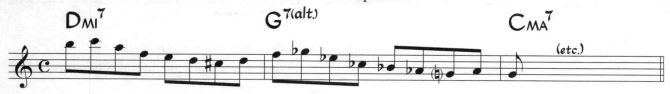

*Long II-V literal tritone replications starting on the #root of the II chord*

Ex.3-91 starts on the #root of the II chord and uses replication up a tritone.

Ex.3-92 also starts on the #root of the II chord and uses replication down a tritone.

Of course there are many more possibilities. I've just shown some demos, two from each starting note, one going up a tritone and one going down a tritone. This should give you all you need to pursue further if you so desire.

*Literal tritone replication of one cell in the middle of long II-V changes*

Sometimes you can use literal tritone replication of just one cell in the middle of the II-V change resulting in a different cell combination in each measure, but still using tritone substitution. To do this the second cell from the first measure is replicated a tritone away in the first half of the second measure, followed by another cell in the "key" of the tritone substitution.

*One cell replication in the middle using cells starting on the root*

Play Ex.3-93.

Look at the middle two cells They start on the roots of Dmi7 and Abmi7 using literal replication up a tritone.

Ex.3-94 also uses cells in the middle that start on the roots of Dmi7 and Abmi7 and use literal replication down a tritone.

*One cell replication in the middle using cells starting on the b3rd*

Ex.3-95 uses cells in the middle that start on the b3rds of Dmi7 and Abmi7 and use literal replication up a tritone.

Ex.3-96 also uses cells in the middle that start on the b3rds of Dmi7 and Abmi7 and use literal replication down a tritone.

*One cell replication in the middle using cells starting on the 5th*

Ex.3-97 uses cells in the middle that start on the 5ths of Dmi7 and Abmi7 and use literal replication up a tritone.

Ex.3-98 also uses cells in the middle that start on the 5ths of Dmi7 and Abmi7 and use literal replication down a tritone.

93

*One cell replication in the middle using cells starting on the b7th*

Ex.3-99 uses cells in the middle that start on the b7ths of Dmi7 and Abmi7 and use literal replication up a tritone.

Ex.3-100 also uses cells in the middle that start on the b7ths of Dmi7 and Abmi7 and use literal replication down a tritone.

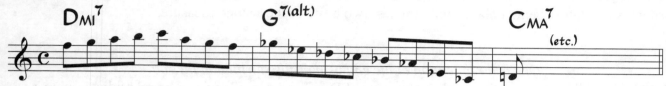

*One cell replication in the middle using cells starting on the 9th*

Ex.3-101 uses cells in the middle that start on the 9ths of Dmi7 and Abmi7 and use literal replication up a tritone.

Ex.3-102 also uses cells in the middle that start on the 9ths of Dmi7 and Abmi7 and use literal replication down a tritone.

*One cell replication in the middle using cells starting on the 11th*

Ex.3-103 uses cells in the middle that start on the 11ths of Dmi7 and Abmi7 and use literal replication up a tritone.

Ex.3-104 also uses cells in the middle that start on the 11ths of Dmi7 and Abmi7 and use literal replication down a tritone.

94

Perhaps you've noticed that I didn't show any one-cell replications starting on the maj7th, the 13th, or the #root. Not all cells work for literal tritone replication. The cells usually have a specific target note, sometimes with an optional choice or two. The way the cells are actually heard when played in combinations is with the strong-beat eighth note completing a four-note group that starts on the "and" after the last strong beat (the strong beats being one and three). For a thorough explanation see Hal Galper's great book, *Forward Motion*. The above-mentioned cells target areas that just don't translate into tritone replication.

*Literal tritone replication of one cell at the end of long II-V changes*
Sometimes you can use literal tritone replication of just one cell at the end of the II-V change resulting in the tritone substitution being delayed until the last two beats of the second measure.

*One cell replication at the end using cells starting on the root*
Ex.3-105 uses cells at the end that start on the roots of Dmi7 and Abmi7 and use literal replication up a tritone.

Ex.3-106 uses cells at the end that start on the roots of Dmi7 and Abmi7 and use literal replication down a tritone.

*One cell replication at the end using cells starting on the b3rd*
Ex.3-107 uses cells at the end that start on the b3rds of Dmi7 and Abmi7 and use literal replication up a tritone.

Ex.3-108 uses cells at the end that start on the b3rds of Dmi7 and Abmi7 and use literal replication down a tritone.

*One cell replication at the end using cells starting on the 5th*

Ex.3-109 uses cells at the end that start on the 5ths of Dmi7 and Abmi7 and use literal replication up a tritone.

Ex.3-110 uses cells at the end that start on the 5ths of Dmi7 and Abmi7 and use literal replication down a tritone.

*One cell replication at the end using cells starting on the b7th*

Ex.3-111 uses cells at the end that start on the b7ths of Dmi7 and Abmi7 and use literal replication up a tritone.

Ex.3-112 uses cells at the end that start on the b7ths of Dmi7 and Abmi7 and use literal replication down a tritone.

*One cell replication at the end using cells starting on the 9th*

Ex.3-113 uses cells at the end that start on the 9ths of Dmi7 and Abmi7 and use literal replication up a tritone.

Ex.3-114 uses cells at the end that start on the 9ths of Dmi7 and Abmi7 and use literal replication down a tritone.

*One cell replication at the end using cells starting on the 11th*

Ex.3-115 uses cells at the end that start on the 11ths of Dmi7 and Abmi7 and use literal replication up a tritone.

Ex.3-116 uses cells at the end that start on the 11ths of Dmi7 and Abmi7 and use literal replication down a tritone.

*Long II-V changes using tritone substitution without replication*

There are probably thousands of possible lines on long II-V changes using tritone substitution that don't use replication, but use just the cells we already know. Naturally I'm not even going to attempt to write them all out, but I'll show a few random examples to give you an idea of how to do it. At some point you should be able to start improvising new combinations on the spot.

Ex.3-117 starts with the same combination as 3-74 but continues with different cells during the tritone substitute bar.

Ex.3-118 starts with the same combination an octave higher and continues with another tritone substitute combination.

Ex.3-119 starts on the root of Dmi7 while the second bar starts on the 5th of the Abmi7 we're superimposing over the G7alt.

Ex.3-120 starts on the 5th of Dmi7 while the second bar starts on the 11th of the Abmi7 we're superimposing over the G7alt.

Ex.3-121 starts on the 11th of Dmi7 while the second bar starts on the 5th of the Abmi7 (the reverse of the last example).

Ex.3-122 starts on the 5th of Dmi7 while the second bar starts on the b3rd of the Abmi7 we're superimposing over the G7alt.

Ex.3-123 starts on the b3rd of Dmi7 while the second bar starts on the root of the Abmi7 we're superimposing over the G7alt.

Ex.3-124 starts on the 9th of Dmi7. The second measure also starts on the 9th of the Abmi7 we're superimposing over the G7alt, but no tritone replication is used.

Ex.3-125 starts on the maj7th of the Dmi7. You can figure out the rest.

Ex.3-126 also starts on the maj7th of the Dmi7 but continues with a different combination.

## Long II-V changes using minor 3rd substitution

In addition to tritone substitution, jazz musicians from the bebop era to the present also frequently use minor 3rd substitution. Using the cells we already know we can play the II chord measure using the cell combinations from the home key and the V chord measure using cell combinations borrowed from the key that's a minor 3rd above the home key. In the key of C this would be Eb, meaning we would use Fmi7-Bb7 cell combinations over the G7. We already touched on the subject in Chapter 1 of my previous book, *Line Games* in the sections called "Applying hexatonics using the 13susb9 sound and its harmonic implications" and "Applying hexatonics to II-V-I in minor tonality." The lines we're about to look at will actually fit any of the harmonic scenarios shown below:

| | | |
|---|---|---|
| Dmi7 | G7susb9 | Cmaj7 |
| Dmi7 | Fmi7-Bb7 | Cmaj7 |
| Fmaj7 | Fmi6 | Cmaj7 |
| Fmaj7 | Bb7 | Cmaj7 |
| Bmi7b5 | E7alt | Ami9 |

Play Ex.3-127.

It demonstrates the minor 3rd substitution. Notice that the first cell of the second bar is the same as the first cell from 3-29 transposed up a minor 3rd, so it can be replaced with likewise transposed cells shown in 3-30, 3-31, and 3-32 for more variations.

### *Long II-V changes using literal minor 3rd replication*
As with tritone substitution, minor 3rd substitution can be clearly demonstrated by using literal replication. The minor 3rd does not divide the octave in half like the tritone does, so first we'll check out literal replications up a minor 3rd. Later we'll look at literal replications down a major 6th, the inversion of up a minor 3rd.

### *Literal up a minor 3rd replications starting on the root of the II chord*
Ex.3-128 begins with the same cell combination as 3-127, then replicates it up a minor 3rd in the second bar.

Ex.3-129 also starts on the root with a familiar combination.

*Literal up a minor 3rd replications starting on the b3rd of the II chord*

Ex.3-130 starts on the b3rd of Dmi7 and uses the same first cell from 3-29 again, so try the variations shown in 3-30, 3-31, and 3-32. Since we're replicating up a minor 3rd the same variations can also be replicated. You should also try mixing different variations in the first and second bars for even more variety.

Ex.3-131 also starts on the b3rd and uses minor 3rd replication.

So does Ex.3-132.

*Literal up a minor 3rd replications starting on the 5th of the II chord*

Ex.3-133 starts on the 5th of the II chord and uses minor 3rd replication.

Ex.3-134 uses a familiar "5th to 3rd" II-V sequence with minor 3rd replication.

*Literal up a minor 3rd replications starting on the 9th of the II chord*

Ex.3-135 starts on the 9th of the II chord and uses minor 3rd replication.

So does Ex.3-136.

*A literal up a minor 3rd replication starting on the 11th of the II chord*

Ex.3-137 starts on the 11th of the II chord and uses minor 3rd replication.

*Long II-V changes using literal down a major 6th replications*

Now let's check out some down a major 6th replications, the inversion of up a minor 3rd. I'm only going to show one demo for each starting note.

*A literal down a major 6th replication starting on the root of the II chord*

Ex.3-138 starts on the root of the II chord and uses down a major 6th replication.

*A literal down a major 6th replication starting on the b3rd of the II chord*

Ex.3-139 starts on the b3rd of the II chord and uses down a major 6th replication. The first cell this time is the one shown in 3-32, a variation, so also practice using the cells shown in 3-30 and 3-31 and also the first cell from 3-29.

*A literal down a major 6th replication starting on the 5th of the II chord*

Ex.3-140 starts on the 5th of the II chord and uses down a major 6th replication.

*A literal down a major 6th replication starting on the 9th of the II chord*

Ex.3-141 starts on the 9th of the II chord and uses down a major 6th replication.

*A literal down a major 6th replication starting on the 11th of the II chord*

Ex.3-142 starts on the 11th of the II chord and uses down a major 6th replication.

*Long II-V changes using minor 3rd substitution without replication*

Many combinations using minor 3rd substitutions without replications are possible, but I'll only show two or three from each starting note to demonstrate a few of the possibilities.

*Minor 3rd substitutions without replications starting on the root of the II chord*

Ex.3-143 shows a combination using minor 3rd substitution without replication starting on the root of the II chord.

Ex.3-144 also starts on the root of the II chord.

*Minor 3rd substitutions without replications starting on the b3rd of the II chord*

Ex.3-145 shows a combination using minor 3rd substitution without replication starting on the b3rd of the II chord.

So does Ex.3-146.

*Minor 3rd substitutions without replications starting on the 5th of the II chord*

Ex.3-147 shows a combination using minor 3rd substitution without replication starting on the 5th of the II chord.

Ex.3-148 also starts on the 5th of the II chord. The combination in the second bar actually comes from Chapter 2.

*Minor 3rd substitutions without replications starting on the 9th of the II chord*

Ex.3-149 shows a combination using minor 3rd substitution without replication starting on the 9th of the II chord.

So does Ex.3-150.

*Minor 3rd substitutions without replications starting on the 11th of the II chord*

Ex.3-151 shows a combination using minor 3rd substitution without replication starting on the 11th of the II chord.

Ex.3-152 also starts on the 11th of the II chord.

So does Ex.3-153.

*Minor 3rd substitutions without replications starting on the 13th of the II chord*

Ex.3-154 shows a combination using minor 3rd substitution without replication starting on the 13th of the II chord.

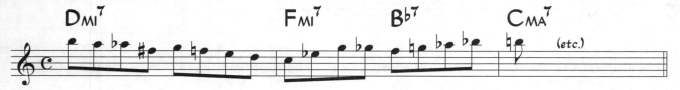

Ex.3-155 also starts on the 13th of the II chord. This time the first bar uses the combination from Chapter 2.

*A minor 3rd substitution without replication starting on the maj7th of the II chord*

Ex.3-156 shows a combination using minor 3rd substitution without replication starting on the maj7th of the II chord.

You may be wondering why none of the examples started from the b7th of the II chord. Keep in mind that the harmonic possibilities for these examples include the relative minor tonality's II-V-I, in this case Bmi7b5-E7alt-Ami. The b7th of Dmi7 is C, very dissonant against Bmi7b5. The b7th of Fmi7 is Eb, also very dissonant against the E7alt. It's not impossible to use those dissonant notes, even on the downbeat, but I opted for a more problem-free approach at this time.

## Combining long II-V changes on the Rhythm changes bridge

As you recall, the bridge in Rhythm changes is a very long (two bars each) dominant cycle. Because there's two full measures of each dom7 chord many jazz musicians will treat each chord as if it were a regular long II-V progression. So, instead of D7-G7-C7-F7, two bars each, we can think Ami7-D7-Dmi7-G7-Gmi7-C7-Cmi7-F7, one bar each. That means we can apply our long II-V lines to the Rhythm changes bridge.

*Rhythm bridges using unaltered II-V combinations that replicate after four bars*

Let's start by using some unaltered long II-V combinations that will replicate down a whole-step after four bars. I'm only going to show the first four bars of each Rhythm bridge, plus the first eighth-note of the fifth bar. Since there's a four bar replication, that last note will always be a whole-step lower than the starting note, as will be the chord changes.

*Unaltered four-bar replications staring on the root of the first II chord*

Ex.3-157 shows the first four bars of a Rhythm bridge using unaltered II-V combinations that starts on the root of the first II chord (Ami7) and can be replicated down a whole-step in the next four bars. The final G note is the start of the replication.

Ex.3-158 also starts on the root of the first II chord. The third bar also happens to start on the root of the second II chord (Dmi7), but it's not a replication.

*Unaltered four-bar replications staring on the b3rd of the first II chord*

The first note of Ex.3-159 is C, the b3rd of Ami7. The final note, Bb, is the b3rd of Gmi7 and again can be used to start a four-bar replication.

Ex.3-160 also starts on the b3rd of the first II chord.

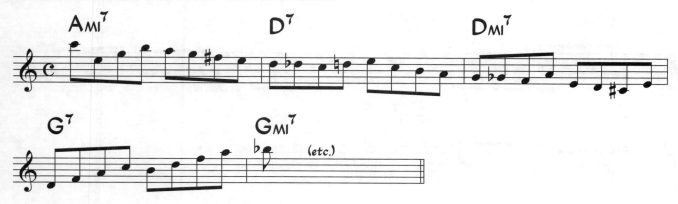

*Unaltered four-bar replications staring on the 5th of the first II chord*

Ex.3-161 starts on the 5th of the first II chord and also can be replicated down a whole-step after the first four bars.

Ex.3-162 also starts on the 5th of the first II chord.

*An unaltered four-bar replication staring on the b7th of the first II chord*

Ex.3-163 shows a four-bar replication line starting on the b7th of the first II chord.

*An unaltered four-bar replication staring on the maj7th of the first II chord*

Ex.3-164 shows a four-bar replication line starting on the maj7th of the first II chord.

*Unaltered four-bar replications staring on the 9th of the first II chord*

Ex.3-165 starts on the 9th of the first II chord and also can be replicated down a whole-step after the first four bars.

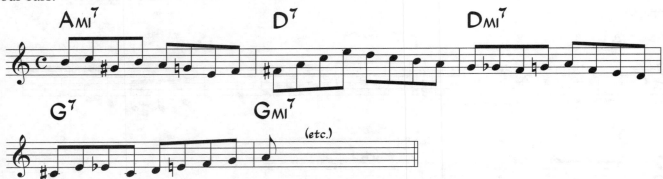

Ex.3-166 also starts on the 9th of the first II chord.

107

*Unaltered four-bar replications staring on the 11th of the first II chord*

Ex.3-167 starts on the 11th of the first II chord and also can be replicated down a whole-step after the first four bars.

Ex.3-168 also starts on the 11th of the first II chord.

*Unaltered four-bar replications staring on the 13th of the first II chord*

Ex.3-169 starts on the 13th of the first II chord and also can be replicated down a whole-step after the first four bars.

Ex.3-170 also starts on the 13th of the first II chord.

*Rhythm bridges using unaltered II-V combinations that replicate after only two bars*

It it also possible to replicate after only two bars when using unaltered combinations. Each two-bar combination will be either a up a fourth or down a fifth from the previous combination, so it will result in a very wide range line that may limit the number of practical possibilities. I'm only going to show two to demonstrate, one going up in fourths and one going down in fifths.

Ex.3-171 shows a two bar combination that's replicated going up in fourths. Work out the next two bars, continuing up in fourths. I know you can do it!

Ex.3-172 shows a two bar combination that's replicated going down in fifths. Work out the next two bars, continuing down in fifths. The range will be even wider, but it is not only possible, but practical as well.

Of course you don't have to use replication at all. You can create many, many new lines out of the relatively few cells we've been using to play long lines through the Rhythm bridge using unaltered II-V combinations. It's up to you to discover and practice some of your favorites.

*Rhythm bridges using tritone substitution combinations that replicate after four bars*

The long II-V changes used on Rhythm bridges can also use tritone substitution. These are especially good for the Bill Evans substitution mentioned above, so I'll use the chord symbols Ami7-D7-Ebmi7-Ab7-Dmi7-G7-Abmi7-Db7-Gmi7 etc. I'm only showing one example, starting from the root, but you should work out several lines starting from each of all the chord degrees and extensions to gain total fluency with the concept.

Ex.3-173 is the demo using tritone substitution with four-bar replication.

You can (and should) work out Rhythm bridges using tritone substitution with two-beat replications and one bar replications and also no replications. Many good combinations are waiting to be discovered and practiced.

*Rhythm bridges using minor 3rd substitution combinations that replicate after four bars*
The long II-V changes used on Rhythm bridges can also use minor 3rd substitution. I'll demonstrate with one example starting on the 9th of the first II chord, Ex.3-174.

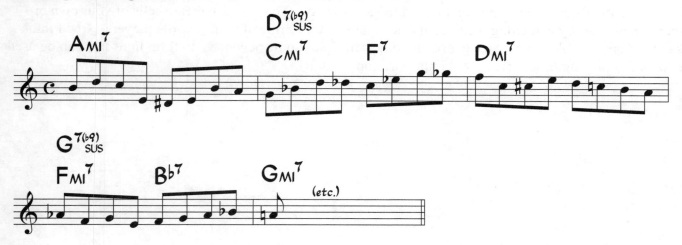

The D7susb9 and G7susb9 chord symbols indicate the harmonies that the line implies. The Cmi7-F7 and Fmi7-Bb7 chord symbols show where the cellular combinations come from. Keep in mind that all the lines we've looked at in this Rhythm bridge section can be used over the standard D7-G7-C7-F7 Rhythm bridge.

*A Rhythm bridge using four bar replication with variations and editing*
The Rhythm bridges using the cellular concept can also be edited and have some rhythmic variations applied. A four bar replication need not be exact, but often works better when the replication has some variations, giving a "question and answer" or "call and response" effect.

110

Ex.3-175 demonstrates this with a full eight bar Rhythm bridge based on the four bar replication example shown in 3-157. The beginning and ending of the first four bars feature combinations of editing and rhythmic variations. The second four begins with a rhythmic variation and the seventh and eighth bars have a variation using tritone substitution. The chord symbols are just the standard D7-G7-C7-F7 Rhythm bridge.

Hopefully the examples have demonstrated that it is possible to improvise many, many different lines using relatively few cells combined and recombined in various ways. You can also create cells of your own or discover new ones by extracting them from solos that you transcribe of your favorite players. Now I think it's time to take a look at how we can use the same cells, plus some new ones, to form lines that can be used for "outside" playing or for "free jazz" improvisation.

# Chapter 4 – "Outside" and "Free" Playing

Playing "outside" doesn't mean you might have to take your umbrella, it means playing lines that are intentionally dissonant against the chord you are soloing over at the time. Likewise, "free" playing doesn't mean you won't get paid for the gig (although that too may be true), it means playing with no set chords or key or form—it's created spontaneously and collectively (if performing with others). "Outside" lines are most commonly used in static harmonic situations, such as one or two chord vamps, a modal section, or a pedal tone (or drone) in the bass, but they can be used during regular chord changes if handled with care. Usually the "outside" line will resolve "inside" or be followed by (and also usually preceded by) "inside" lines, creating long tension-resolution effects. They should end up sounding surprising and logical at the same time. Let's check out some actual recorded examples.

*Some actual recorded examples using cells for "outside" improvisation*

Play Ex.4-1.

It's from the same famous McCoy Tyner solo we used at the beginning of the triad-pair chapter from my previous book *Line Games*, where McCoy uses the Eb-F major whole-step pair to create some great "inside" lines over the static F7sus. Ex.4-1 begins with McCoy playing the F note, then hinting at an Ab triad going down to a Gb triad, forming a whole-step pair that implies a change from the F mixolydian mode into an F phrygian mode. This is followed by another major whole-step pair, E and D, implying E mixolydian, which is completely foreign to the F root. It's the original mode down a half-step (up or down a half-step is often called "side-slipping"). After playing a cell with a C# note, the 6th of E mixolydian, in the next bar McCoy returns to F phrygian with a line that can be analyzed as the Ab-Gb major pair or as Eb minor pentatonic. In the last bar McCoy resolves beautifully back into F7sus. It's interesting that the triad-pairs formed a series of triads descending in whole-steps, Ab-Gb-E-D, suggesting the possibility that melodic cells descending in whole-steps might be useful for "outside" playing.

Now play Ex.4-2.

This is from later in the same McCoy solo. This time he jumps right in with F phrygian. The first two cells are both permutations of a 1-b3-4-5 fragment from Eb minor pentatonic. The next cell is 5-4-b3-1 from E *natural* minor pentatonic (a half-step from Eb minor, implying another "side-slip"). The following cell reveals that the second bar is from a Gmaj7-Emi7 hexatonic scale (G-A-B-D-E-F#), totally foreign to the F root. The next two cells suggest Eb minor pentatonic descending to Db minor pentatonic. The last six notes spell out a Cb major-Ab minor pentatonic scale, the b5-b6-b7-b9-#9 of F7. Being later in the solo than the previous example, McCoy doesn't resolve the line right away as he's building more tension as the solo develops.

Ex.4-3 comes from a tenor saxophone solo recorded by Michael Brecker.

This example demonstrates a very sophisticated application of the cellular approach to "outside" playing. There is a cell combination that is actually ten notes long which is replicated twice in descending major 3rds. This is an excerpt from a longer line and starts inside, moves outside, moves back inside in the middle, and then goes back out. The first ten note replicated phrase starts on beat four in the the first bar. Being ten notes long, the replicated fragment cannot be all four-note cells. I imagine that the first four-note cell has a two-note extension, forming a six-note cell that is followed by a four-note cell, totaling ten notes. These ten notes are a Cbmaj7-Abmi7 hexatonic scale, somewhat "out" on F7, followed by a replication down a major 3rd, Gmaj7-Emi7 hexatonic, very "out" on the Cmi7 chord, but when replicated down a major 3rd it becomes Ebmaj7-Cmi7 hexatonic, very "inside." The line ends with another Cbmaj7-Abmi7 hexatonic line.

Ex.4-4 comes from the same Michael Brecker solo.

This line starts inside the Cmi7 sound with some bebop cells using some standard chromaticism. On the fourth beat of the first bar a four-note cell is played which is then replicated many times descending in minor 3rds. It starts kind of out and weaves in and out as it descends.

*Principles of "outside" improvisation*

If you continue to check out lines by Tyner and Brecker along with lines by other players using similar approaches such as Jerry Bergonzi, Hal Galper, Woody Shaw, Larry Young, David Liebman, Joe Diorio, John Scofield and Mike Stern, you'll find that cells and cell combinations can be "side-slipped" up or down a half-step and back, or moved up or down chromatically, or up or down in whole-steps, or up or down in minor 3rds, or up or down in major 3rds, or up or down in 4ths, or up or down in tritones. Combinations of these also occur, such as down a major 3rd followed by down a minor 3rd, or up a minor 3rd followed by up or down a half-step. They can start in and go out and back in, or start out and go in and back out, or start in and go out, or start out and go in. The inside-outside-inside scheme is the easiest to hear and understand, so most of our examples will use that scheme. For a thorough explanation of the theory behind outside improvisation, see *The Jazz Theory Book* by Mark Levine. In general, simple cells without chromatic embellishments work best, including lines from hexatonic scales and hexatonic triad-pairs, and lines derived from basic pentatonic scales are especially effective.

## "Side-slipping"

The term "side-slipping" usually refers to playing out by going up or down a half-step from the chord you're soloing on, so it's an easy way (especially on guitar) to get introduced to outside improvisation. Actually, one of the chromatic embellishment cells we've already been using a lot can be re-analyzed as a side-slip.

Ex.4-5 is the familiar cell, starting on the major 7th of Cmi7 and resolving to the root after using a double-chromatic approach from above and a return to the half-step below.

Ex.4-6 shows the same line re-written using a C# instead of a Db, making it a simple 1-b3-2-1 cell on Bmi7, down a half-step from the C. The Bmi7 chord symbol is for analysis only.

Ex.4-7 shows a typical line using the cell inside of a Cmi7 line similar to how we've already used it.

If side-slipping can be down or *up* a half-step, we should be able to use the same 1-b3-2-1 cell from C#mi7, up a half-step, as well. Ex.4-8 shows the same line, but with the Bmi7 cell replaced with the C#mi7 cell.

Since the down a half-step version doubles as an inside embellishment, it sounds a lot tamer than the up a half-step version, which clearly sounds "out."

*The basic pentatonic scale*

I mentioned that cells derived from basic pentatonic scales are especially effective for outside improvisation. Why should this be so? Let's take a look.

Play Ex.4-9, one octave of a basic Eb major pentatonic scale.

It's 1-2-3-5-6-8 (or 1) of a major scale, or it can be seen as an Eb major scale with the 4th and 7th left out. The 4th and the 7th form the only tritone in the key, plus they're both involved in the two half-steps found in the key. This means the pentatonic scale has no tritone and no half-steps or leading tones, so the scale is very open and consonant.

Now play Ex.4-10.

This is the same Eb pentatonic scale but with the notes re-arranged. They're spread out to show that all the notes are related to each other by the interval of a perfect 5th. The 5th is the strongest and most consonant interval after the unison and the octave.

Next play Ex.4-11.

This is Eb pentatonic again, but arranged in perfect 4ths this time. The perfect 4th is the inversion of the perfect 5th, so it's only natural.

These 5th and 4th relationships of the notes in the pentatonic scale means that cells derived from it will be highly resonant, creating their own powerful harmonic field. This is great for outside playing because, as Mark Levine points out, most outside playing is really *bi-tonality*, or two different tonalities played at the same time. We haven't yet looked at deriving cells from pentatonic scales, so now is the time.

The key of Eb was chosen because the recorded examples we looked at were over either F7sus or Cmi7-F7, which the Eb major pentatonic fits. If you start the Eb major pentatonic scale on the C note, you will hear the ever-popular C minor pentatonic scale. If you start on F, it's an F9sus chord. The F9sus is actually symmetrical. The intervals going up from F and down from F are the same. Notice that F is in the center of both the stack-of-5ths example and the stack-of-4ths example, showing it to be the axis of symmetry for the scale.

Ex.4-12 shows a pattern consisting of all the consecutive four-note cells in our pentatonic scale, ascending and descending.

Ex.4-13 shows a fragment from a rhythmically displaced version of the last pattern. This forms a fresh set of four-note cells with one note repeated. Work out the entire exercise because we will be using the cells from this displaced version.

Ex.4-14 skips notes in the scale and actually can be seen as generating two-note cells, but two plus two equals four.

Ex.4-15 reverses the direction of each second skip, creating actual four-note cells.

116

Ex.4-16 reverses the direction of each first skip, resulting in a complimentary set of four-note cells.

These last two examples can also be displaced by one beat to yield other cells we'll be using.

*Side-slipping using the new cells*

Ex.4-17 is based on the descending portion of 4-12. The first bar is the first two cells untouched. The second bar side-slips up a half-step.

Ex.4-18 is the same as the last example except this time the side-slip is down a half-step.

Ex.4-19 uses the descending portion of 4-16 displaced by one beat. The side-slip is up a half step and uses the same trick used in 4-17.

Ex.4-20 is like 4-19 but side-slips down a half step. Use the same technique used in 4-18.

*More pentatonic four-note cells and cell combinations*

Ex.4-21 derives three more four-note cells from our pentatonic scale by arpeggiating the three sus4 triads found in the scale. They are Csus, Fsus, and Bbsus. They are shown ascending and descending.

Ex.4-22 alternates cells from the ascending portion of 4-17 with the ascending cells from 4-22, producing new combinations.

Ex.4-23 combines cells from 4-14 with descending cells from 4-21. The last cell is the first descending cell from 4-21 played down an octave.

Ex.4-24 combines cells from the ascending portion of 4-14 with descending cells from 4-12.

*Side-slipping using the new combinations*

Ex.4-25 uses the first combination from 4-23 and applies both up a half-step and down a half-step side-slips. You can work out other similar side-slip lines using the other combinations from 4-23.

118

Ex.4-26 is based on 4-24 with the second bar side-slipped up a half-step.

Ex.4-27 is based on 4-24 with the second bar side-slipped down a half-step.

*Beyond the four-note cell with some seven-note cells*

Ex.4-28 shows some seven-note cells based on the three three-note stacks of perfect 4ths found in our pentatonic scale. The first two notes are used as pick-up notes to the following measure.

*Side-slipping the seven-note cells*

The first seven-note cell from 4-28 is used in Ex.4-29 in a similar fashion as 4-25 using both up and down side-slips. You can work out other similar side-slip lines using the other seven-note cells from 4-28.

*Five-note cells implying a 6/8 cross-rhythm*

Ex.4-30 shows some five-note cells that are actually six eighth-notes long, creating a 6/8 cross-rhythm.

*Side-slipping the five-note cross-rhythm cells*

Ex.4-31 side-slips the first five-note 6/8 cross-rhythm cell from 4-30 both up and down as in 4-25 and 4-29. It finishes with a combination of familiar cells.

*Four-note cells implying a 5/8 cross-rhythm*

Ex.4-32 is based on the descending four-note cells from 4-13, but lengthened in time by one eighth-note to create a 5/8 cross-rhythm.

*Side-slipping the 5/8 cross-rhythm cells*

Ex.4-33 is patterned after 4-17 with the 5/8 cross-rhythm applied. You can also do it with a down side-slip.

## Extended or consecutive side-slipping up or down chromatically

Many of the lines demonstrating outside playing are sequences that use exact replication of cells or cell combinations. It's the easiest way to start going out because when we start with a cell or combination that's inside and then replicate it outside of the key the replication makes it sound logical in spite of the "wrong" notes. The easiest way to start getting beyond simple side-slipping up or down a half-step is to keep sequencing the replication moving further away from the home key by consecutive half-steps up or down. You can go as far as you like, but the following examples will only go a short distance before reversing direction and returning "home" in half-steps, the easiest way to resolve this type of line.

120

Ex.4-33 demonstrates with a simple cell ascending in half-steps, then descending. A variation of the cell occurs at the end of the third bar, then a reversed version of the variation as the line resolves.

Ex.4-35 starts with the reversed variation and descends in half-steps before returning.

Ex.4-36 uses a cell from the ascending portion of 4-14 when going up and a cell from the descending portion of 4-14 when returning. The resolution uses a different cell to form a variation that helps release the tension created by the chromatic sequences.

Ex.4-37 uses a mixture of cells and also uses a similar variation for the resolution.

Ex.4-38 shows a familiar combination going up in half-steps, then returning. There's a slight variation at the end.

Your assignment is to try the above combination descending in half-steps and returning, then try other combinations you like ascending and descending.

## Sequencing up and down in whole-steps

Other consecutive intervals besides half-steps can be used to create sequences that go out. The half-step and the tritone instantly create the maximum amount of dissonance. The whole-step creates very little if any dissonance, but if consecutive whole-steps are used the dissonance increases the closer the sequence gets to the tritone. I'm only going to demonstrate using one familiar cell combination, but you should also try other cell combinations and single cells as well.

Ex.4-39 is a familiar combination replicated up twice in whole-steps followed by a different cell to resolve.

Ex.4-40 is the same combination going down in whole-steps. It also uses a different cell to resolve.

## Sequencing down and up in minor 3rds

*Sequencing down in minor 3rds*

Ex.4-41 is a familiar cell sequenced down in minor 3rds.

Ex.4-42 uses something a little different. The relative major of C minor is Eb, so this example sequences the *keys* of Eb major to C major to A major to F# major and back to Eb major, descending in minor 3rds over the Cmi7 or F7sus. Different cells are used on each key.

122

Ex.4-43 also uses the relative major descending in minor 3rds, but a replicated triadic cell this time.

Ex.4-44 uses an excerpt from the Brecker line shown in 4-4 that starts and ends inside and descends in minor 3rds.

*Sequencing up in minor 3rds*

Ex.4-45 uses the same chromatic cell used in 4-44, but ascending in minor 3rds this time.

Ex.4-46 uses the same triadic cells used in 4-43, but ascending in minor 3rds this time.

Ex.4-47 uses our familiar seven-note cell from 4-28 ascending in minor 3rds.

# Sequencing down and up in major 3rds

Going up or down a major 3rd takes you quickly to a place that it takes two consecutive whole-steps to get to. Major 3rds divide the octave into three equal parts and they avoid sounding like the more typical minor 3rd or tritone substitutions frequently used for "inside" playing. This makes them sound fresh and surprising, yet still logical.

*Sequencing down in major 3rds*

Ex.4-48 sequences the familiar 1-2-3-5 (b3-4-5-b7 in C minor) Eb major cell down in major 3rds.

Ex.4-49 reverses the order of notes inside each cell, still descending in major 3rds.

Ex.4-50 uses yet another permutation of the same notes.

Ex.4-51 starts a melodic sequence with two cells from Eb major-C minor pentatonic and continues the sequence with two cells from Cb major-Ab minor pentatonic, then two from G major-E minor pentatonic before retuning to the home key.

Ex.4-52 uses a similar scheme but with different cells forming a different melodic sequence.

124

Ex.4-53 shows an interesting variation of the scheme.

One cell of a melodic sequence comes from Eb major-C minor pentatonic followed by two from Cb major-Ab minor pentatonic, then two from G major-E minor pentatonic before retuning to one cell in the home key. This causes the changes of key to happen in the middle of each bar instead of at the more predictable bar lines.

Ex.4-54 is based on the same scheme variation used in 4-53 but with different cells forming a different melodic sequence.

Ex.4-55 shows a familiar two cell combination replicated down in major 3rds.

Ex.4-56 shows another familiar two cell combination replicated down in major 3rds.

*Sequencing up in major 3rds*

Ex.4-57 uses the same type of cell used in 4-48 but going up in major 3rds.

Ex.4-58 uses the same notes as 4-57 but the permutations keep changing, making it less predictable. This idea follows the McCoy examples above.

*Sequences that go down a major 3rd, then back up a major 3rd*

A line using a major 3rd sequence need not go to all three keys that are major thirds apart. Some very effective outside lines can be created by going up or down a major 3rd, then returning home without the consecutive major 3rds. On minor chords my personal favorites go down a major 3rd, then back home up a major 3rd.

Ex.4-59 is based on the scheme variation used in 4-53 with one home key cell followed by two down a major 3rd, then returning home with the key changes in the middle of each bar. The permutations change for melodic variety.

Ex.4-60 uses a familiar cell combination replicated down a major 3rd, then resolving.

Ex.4-61 shows another familiar two cell combination replicated down a major 3rd, then resolving.

*Some whole-tone patterns good for mixing with major 3rd sequences*

Since all the 3rds in a whole-tone scale are major 3rds, whole-tone patterns can generate some new cells and cell combinations that can be used together with major 3rd sequences.

Ex.4-62 shows a line that was actually used by Wes Montgomery over a mi7 chord (although Wes' was in a different key).

126

It's a string of augmented triads going up the whole-tone scale from B natural. The scale doesn't even have the root of the Cmi7 in it. If it did, it would have an E natural and a G#, making it much more difficult to use in this situation.

Ex.4-63 shows a typical descending whole-tone scale sequence.

Parts of the pattern suggest a C melodic minor tonality and other parts suggest a C phrygian mode.

Ex.4-64 is a line combining some whole-tone cells inside of a down-a-major 3rd, back-up-a-major 3rd sequence.

The first five notes are from C minor pentatonic. The next eight notes are a two cell combination from Ab minor pentatonic, displaced by one eighth-note. This is followed by a two cell whole-tone combination extracted from 4-63, also displaced by one eighth-note. Then there are three displaced four-note cells from Ab minor pentatonic followed by a resolution back to C minor.

*An ascending major 3rd sequence suggesting the augmented scale*

Play Ex.4-65.

If you think of the relative major of Cminor, Eb major, it's easy to recognize the four cells as simple arpeggios of Ebmaj7-Gmaj7-Bmaj7-Ebmaj7, ascending in major 3rds. They are also b3-5-b7-9 arpeggios of Cmi9-Emi9-G#mi9-Cmi9. If you reduce the number of notes used in the line by making enharmonic notes the same (which they are), you'll see that only six notes are used. The Eb and the D# are enharmonic. The Bb and the A# are also the same. The six resulting notes form what is usually called the augmented scale. This suggests that the augmented scale and its melodic patterns and sequences should be a good source of cells for major 3rd sequences, so let's check it out.

*The augmented scale*

Ex.4-66 shows an Eb augmented scale.

I chose Eb because Cmi-maj7 and F9#11 both contain an Eb augmented triad (Eb+). The scale is actually a hexatonic triad-pair consisting of Eb+ and D+, as shown in the example.

The augmented triad is symmetrical, dividing the octave into three equal parts, so naturally the augmented scale is also symmetrical. Therefore each augmented scale is actually three augmented scales, so there are really only four different augmented scales (Eb+=G+=B+, E+=G#+=C+, F+=A+=Db+, and F#+=Bb+=D+).

The Eb augmented scale is also G augmented and B augmented. Notice that these notes are the roots of the major 7th chords used in example 7-66. Even though  the scale is made out of symmetrical augmented triads, when two a half-step apart are combined it produces many varied and interesting chords. From each of the root notes Eb, G, and B you can find major triads, minor triads, maj7 chords, mi-maj7 chords, maj7#5 chords, and mi-maj7#5 chords to name a few.

*Some augmented scale melodic sequences*

Ex.4-67 ascends like 4-65 but starting on Bmaj7. It descends with a pattern inspired by Joe Diorio. The first descending cell is a permutation of an Ebmaj7 arpeggio, 1-5-3-7. This cell is then sequenced down in major 3rds.

Ex.4-68 uses major triadic cells ascending and descending in major 3rds (continued on following page).

Ex.4-69 uses minor triadic cells ascending and descending in major 3rds.

Ex.4-70 is a popular descending sequence of major triad cells inspired by Oliver Nelson.

In Ex.4-71 each ascending four-note cell could be described as a root-position mi-maj7#5 arpeggio. That would make the first cell a Bmi-maj7#5, but it could also be heard as first-inversion G major triad arpeggio with an added minor third (or #9) on top. The descending half of the exercise is the same as the ascending half, but reversed.

Ex.4-72 is perfect 5ths going up in major 3rds, resulting in the intervallic sequence of up-a-fifth, down-a-minor-third, up-a-fifth, down-a-minor-third, etc. It's reversed descending.

Ex.4-73 is major 7ths going up in major 3rds, resulting in the intervallic sequence of up-a-maj7, down-a-fifth, up-a-maj7, down-a-fifth, etc.

Ex.4-74 is based on 4-72 with the 5ths converted into four-note cells by adding a chromatic lower-neighbor to the bottom note of each 5th.

Ex 4-75 is based on 4-73 with the major 7ths converted into four-note cells by adding a chromatic lower-neighbor to the bottom note of each major 7th.

Ex.4-76 is a pattern that skips over two scale tones of the augmented scale from each step. If you skip over just one scale tone from each step you get all major 3rds, not as interesting, but check them out on your own if you like.

Ex.4-77 reverses the second half of each four-note cell from 4-76. Only the first three cells are shown. Please continue all the way up and back down.

Ex.4-78 reverses the first half of each four-note cell from 4-76. Again, only the first three cells are shown. Continue all the way up and back down.

Ex.4-79 starts a half-step higher than 4-76 and can be seen as a "mirror image" of that pattern.

Ex.4-80 shows the "mirror image" of 4-77.

Ex.4-81 shows the "mirror image" of 4-78.

Ex.4-82 is a pattern that skips over four scale tones of the augmented scale from each step.

Ex.4-83 reverses the second half of each four-note cell from 4-82. Only the first three cells are shown. Continue all the way up and back down.

Ex.4-84 reverses the first half of each four-note cell from 4-82. Again, only the first three cells are shown. Continue all the way up and back down.

Ex.4-85 starts a half-step higher than 4-82 and can be seen as a "mirror image" of that pattern.

Ex.4-86 shows the "mirror image" of 4-83.

Ex.4-87 shows the "mirror image" of 4-84.

Ex.4-88 shows ascending and descending three-note cells creating a cross-rhythm in 4/4 time. Each cell could be a 1-b3-maj7 arpeggio (reversed descending).

Ex.4-89 shows another variation using three-note cells that can be 1-#5-maj7 arpeggios (again, reversed descending).

Ex.4-90 uses three-note cells that are root-position major triad arpeggios ascending and descending in minor 6ths, the inversion of major 3rds.

Ex.4-91 uses three-note cells that are root-position minor triad arpeggios ascending and descending in minor 6ths, the inversion of major 3rds.

Ex.4-92 shows perfect 5ths ascending and descending in minor 6ths, creating the intervallic sequence of up-a-fifth, up-a-half-step, up-a-fifth, up-a-half-step, etc. (reversed descending).

132

Ex.4-93 shows another pattern inspired by Joe Diorio, perfect 4ths ascending and descending in minor 6ths, creating the intervallic sequence of up-a-fourth, up-a-minor 3rd, up-a-fourth, up-a-minor 3rd, etc. (reversed descending).

Ex.4-94 starts a half-step higher than 4-93 and can be seen as the "mirror image" of 4-93, up-a-minor 3rd, up-a-fourth, up-a-minor 3rd, up-a-fourth, etc. (reversed descending).

Your homework assignment is to create combinations of 4-93 and 4-94. Try going up the first measure of 4-94 then descend the first measure of 4-93 reversed. Next go up the first measure of 4-93 then descend the first measure of 4-94 reversed.

Ex.4-95 shows a line using an interesting sequence that's fourteen notes long, starting on beat four of the the first bar. It's all augmented scale. I'll leave the analysis up to you.

## Sequencing up in 4ths

Moving cells up perfect 4ths results in patterns that sound like fast-moving cycles, so I won't show many since so many have already been shown. I will show a few to demonstrate their application to playing outside over static harmony.

Ex.4-96 shows the familiar 1-2-3-5 cell used to imply the cycle Bb-Eb-Ab-Db superimposed over Cmi7 or F7sus. It ends with an inside resolution cell.

Ex.4-97 uses a familiar 3rd-oriented arpeggiated dominant cycle implying Bb7-Eb7-Ab7-Db7 with a resolution cell at the end.

Ex.4-98 uses familiar triadic cells to imply the Bb-Eb-Ab-Db cycle followed by another resolution cell.

## Sequencing in tritones

The following tritone sequences were, for me personally, all inspired by the writings and recordings of jazz guitar genius Joe Diorio.

Ex.4-99 is a three-note 4th chord arpeggio played as a four-note cell ascending in tritones.

Ex.4-100 is a three-note 4th chord arpeggio played as a four-note cell descending in tritones.

If you build a four-note stack of perfect 4ths from C, the top note will be Eb. In Ex.4-101 the Eb is lowered by an octave and comes before the other three notes. The resulting four-note cell is sequenced up in tritones.

Ex.4-102 uses a six-note cell ascending in tritones. The cell is based on a familiar bebop lick based on the Cmi6-Ami7b5 arpeggio.

134

Ex.4-103 is based on displaced hexatonic scales featuring some triad-pairs. The first four notes are from Abmaj7-Fmi7 hexatonic. The next six notes are Dmaj7-Bmi7 hexatonic divided into a Bminor-Amajor triad-pair. The last seven notes are a sequence down another tritone, Abmaj7-Fmi7 hexatonic divided into an Fminor-Ebmajor triad-pair.

Ex.4-104 also uses a six-note cell. Three notes descend in perfect 5ths, then invert and ascend in perfect 4ths (for chordal versions of the same idea see pages 148 and 149 of my earlier book *Three-Note Voicings and Beyond,* Sher Music Co.). The resulting six-note cell is sequenced down in tritones.

## Some interval combinations

As mentioned earlier, cells can also be sequenced in combinations of different intervals. Let's take a cell combination that we previously sequenced in various intervals and try it with an interval combination.

Ex.4-105 shows the familiar cell combination, first replicated down a major 3rd, then replicated again down a minor 3rd from the first replication.

Ex.4-106 is based on a major chord sequence I learned from trumpeter Donald Byrd, down-a-minor 3rd, down-a-half-step, down-a-minor 3rd, down-a-half-step, etc. I discovered that the combination works great for outside playing. The combination starts, after the pick-up notes, with a cell implying Eb major, the relative of C minor. This is followed by a string of cells implying C major, B major, Ab major, G major, and E major before returning to the Eb major.

Ex.4-107 is based on the Michael Brecker line shown in 4-3. Here it's been modified to start and end in C minor. Earlier we analyzed it as hexatonics descending in major 3rds. Let's take a closer look. The first four notes are from Eb major-C minor pentatonic. The next six notes are from Bb major-G minor pentatonic, down a fourth and completing the ten note sequence. The next four notes are from Cb major- Ab minor pentatonic, up a half-step from the last tonality, followed by six notes from Gb major-Eb minor pentatonic, down another fourth. The pattern continues with notes from G major-E minor pentatonic, up another half-step, etc. until the line resolves, so it's actually another interval combination.

Ex.4-108 freely uses displaced cells and cells of various lengths along with free interval combinations to weave in and out of the C minor tonality. I'll leave the detailed analysis up to you.

While we're on the subject of outside improvisation, let's move on and explore some lines derived from different, non-cellular concepts. Of course any line can be sliced up to make cells, but the following lines are generated without a cellular concept in mind.

# Chapter 5 — More 'Outside' Lines:
## 'All Purpose Licks,' including Chromatic Intervals, Serial Tone-Rows, and 23rd Chords

In this chapter we'll explore various new ways to play outside, including playing intervals moving parallel up and down the chromatic scale, and various types of serial tone-rows, meaning that all twelve tones occur in a series before any note gets repeated. One type of tone-row is a chord arpeggio containing all twelve notes, outlining what can be called a 23rd chord. Most of the lines can be thought of as "all purpose licks" because they can usually be used anywhere at any time if done tastefully and with intention.

*Some recorded examples using chromatic intervals*

Play Ex.5-1.

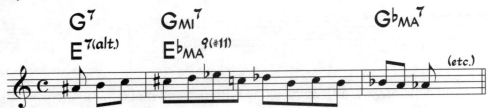

This line is from a Miles Davis trumpet solo. Notice there are two different sets of chord changes. That's because he played the same line two different times in the solo and over different parts of the form, demonstrating the "all purpose" nature of the line.

Ex.5-2 is a similar fragment from the same solo.

In ex.5-3, Miles plays some major 2nds descending chromatically.

Ex.5-4 shows another Miles line using chromatically descending major 2nds.

Ex.5-5 shows guitarist Mike Stern playing a very similar type of line.

*Some recorded examples using serial tone-rows*

Play Ex.5-6.

This wild line comes from a very up-tempo Mike Stern solo on a standard tune. Notice that the first twelve notes are all the notes in the chromatic scale, and the next twelve has them happening again. The line is composed of ascending and descending perfect 5ths going down by whole-steps.

Ex.5-7 shows Mike using perfect 4ths going down by whole-steps. Again, notice that all twelve notes happen before any repeats.

Ex.5-8 comes from another Mike Stern solo on a blues in F using another serial tone row of 4ths going down by whole-steps.

*Some other recorded examples using "all purpose licks"*

Ex.5-9 also is from a Mike Stern solo on a blues in F. The three-note minor 3rd figure climbs in whole-steps and uses all twelve tones before reaching the higher F after three bars.

Try Ex.5-10.

This is an excerpt from a famous solo break recorded by Pat Metheny. It features several segments of major 3rds descending chromatically mixed in with some other intervals.

Ex.5-11 shows another Pat Metheny line that clearly demonstrates his fondness for chromatically descending major 3rds.

## Chromatic interval studies

### Chromatic major 2nds

Ex.5-12 shows the chromatic major 2nds ascending and descending.

Once you learn the basic study you can experiment with creating variations by reversing the direction of some of the intervals. You can try reversing every other interval, but it might be more interesting to do some random asymmetrical patterns. This also applies to all the following intervals.

### Chromatic minor 3rds

An early pioneer of chromatic "all purpose licks" was pianist Art Tatum, who sometimes used chromatically ascending minor 3rds over many types of chords and chord changes. The studies shown here are written in eighth-notes, but Tatum usually played them as triplets creating an interesting cross-rhythm, so you should try all the eighth-note studies in this chapter in triplets as well.

Ex.5-13 shows enough of the notes to work out chromatic minor 3rds.

(etc., up and back down)

*Chromatic major 3rds*

Ex.5-14 shows enough of the notes to work out chromatic major 3rds.

*Chromatic perfect 4ths*

Ex.5-15 shows enough of the notes to work out chromatic perfect 4ths.

*Chromatic tritones*

Ex.5-16 shows enough of the notes to work out chromatic tritones.

*Chromatic perfect 5ths*

These next five examples will start on the note B.

Ex.5-17 shows enough of the notes to work out chromatic perfect 5ths.

140

*Chromatic minor 6ths*

Ex.5-18 shows enough of the notes to work out chromatic minor 6ths.

*Chromatic major 6ths*

Ex.5-19 shows enough of the notes to work out chromatic major 6ths.

*Chromatic minor 7ths*

Ex.5-20 shows enough of the notes to work out chromatic minor 7ths.

*Chromatic major 7ths*

Ex.5-21 shows enough of the notes to work out chromatic major 7ths.

# Serial tone-rows, part 1: Non whole-tone intervals moving in whole-tones

As previously mentioned, a serial tone-row is a line that uses all twelve notes of the chromatic scale before repeating. The two whole-tone scales contain all twelve notes, so one way to produce a serial tone-row is to move any interval that doesn't occur in the whole-tone scale up or down by whole-steps. The non whole-tone intervals are the minor 3rd, the perfect 4th, the perfect 5th, the major 6th, and the major 7th (the inversion of the minor 2nd). Several of the Mike Stern examples shown earlier are perfect examples of this technique.

*Minor 3rds going up and down by whole-steps*

Ex.5-22 shows minor 3rds ascending and descending in whole-steps.

Ex.5-23 shows the same minor 3rds alternating from up to down.

Ex.5-24 shows the same minor 3rds alternating from down to up.

Ex.5-25 demonstrates a possible improvised line using a portion of the tone-row created by minor 3rds ascending in whole-steps.

*Perfect 4ths going up and down by whole-steps*

Ex.5-26 shows perfect 4ths ascending and descending in whole-steps.

Ex.5-27 shows the same perfect 4ths alternating from up to down.

Ex.5-28 shows the same perfect 4ths alternating from down to up.

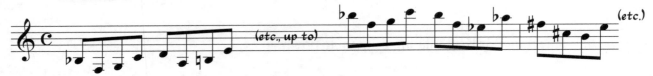

Ex.5-29 demonstrates a possible improvised line using the tone-row created by perfect 4ths descending in whole-steps.

*Perfect 5ths going up and down by whole-steps*

Ex.5-30 shows perfect 5ths ascending and descending in whole-steps.

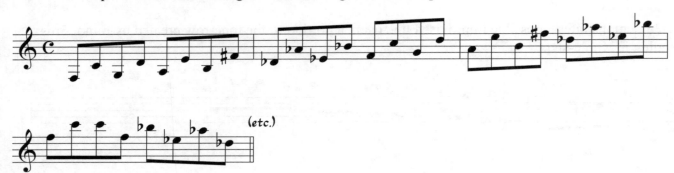

Ex.5-31 shows the same perfect 5ths alternating from up to down.

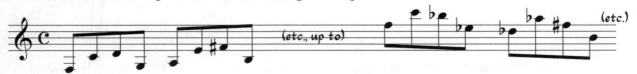

Ex.5-32 shows the same perfect 5ths alternating from down to up.

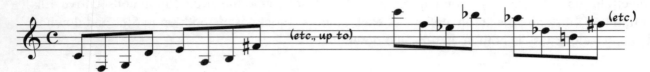

Ex.5-33 demonstrates a possible improvised line using the tone-row created by perfect 5ths descending in whole-steps.

*Major 6ths going up and down by whole-steps*

Ex.5-34 shows major 6ths ascending and descending in whole-steps.

Using the examples above, work out the whole-step 6ths alternating from up to down and from down to up and try using them in improvised lines.

*Major 7ths going up and down by whole-steps*

Ex.5-35 shows major 7ths ascending and descending in whole-steps.

Again your assignment is to work out the whole-step major 7ths alternating from up to down and from down to up and try using them in improvised lines.

## Serial tone-rows, part 2: Consecutive 4ths and 5ths

Since the circle of fifths has all twelve notes, another easy way to create a serial tone-row is to go clockwise around the circle (up in consecutive 5ths), or counter-clockwise around the circle (up in consecutive 4ths). Keep in mind that 4ths and 5ths are inversions of each other, so clockwise is both up in 5ths and down in 4ths and counter-clockwise is both up in 4ths and down in 5ths.

### *Ascending in consecutive perfect 4ths*

Let's start by going up consecutive perfect 4ths. Since the range will probably end up being to wide, we'll have to break it up. Let's break it up into two groups of six to get all twelve notes of the tone-row.

Play Ex.5-36.

It arbitrarily starts on low G and ascends in perfect 4ths. If we went up another 4th from the Ab it would be Db, so the second half of the row starts from C#, then continues for the remaining notes. All twelve notes are used. Up another 4th from the last D note would take us back to a G.

### *Perfect 4ths going down by whole-steps revisited*

In Ex.5-37 up a 4th is followed by its inversion, down a 5th. Then the pattern continues, resulting in a chain of ascending perfect 4ths descending by whole-steps.

Notice that the first note is G again, and the first twelve notes are the same notes in the same order as seen in Ex.5-36. We can derive a rule: groups of two notes ascending in 4ths descend by whole-steps to create a consecutive 4th serial tone-row.

### *Groups of three notes ascending in 4ths*

Ex.5-38 shows the first six notes from 5-36 with the last three notes lowered by an octave, breaking the line into two groups of three.

Notice that the the first note of the second group, Bb, is a minor 3rd higher than the starting note, G. From this we can derive another rule: groups of three notes ascending in 4ths ascend by minor 3rds to create a consecutive 4th serial tone-row.

### Combining groups of three with groups of two

Ex.5-39 starts with three-note groups ascending by minor 3rds going up. When it gets to the top it switches to two-note groups descending by whole-steps all the way back down.

Notice the repeat sign at the end, suggesting that the study can be used as a practice loop.

### Reversing the direction

All the examples shown so far go counter-clockwise around the circle of 5ths. We can also go around clockwise by playing a study in reverse order. Ex.5-40 shows a reversed version of 5-39.

It begins ascending 5ths going up by whole-steps and back down descending 4ths in three-note groups descending by minor 3rds.

Ex.5-41 has three ascending 4th intervals followed by three descending 5th intervals. Then the pattern repeats to get all twelve notes.

Ex.5-42 is the reversed version of 5-41.

Ex.5-43 uses a more elaborate scheme.

Four notes ascend in 4ths followed by one descending 5th, then three notes ascend in 4ths followed by one descending 5th, then two notes ascend by a 4th followed by one descending 5th, then it's back to three, and so on. I'll leave the rest of the analysis up to you.

Ex.5-44 is the reversed version of 5-43.

### Five-note groupings

Alternating between three ascending 4th intervals and two descending 5th intervals produces five-note groupings that climb up by half-steps.

Ex.5-45 shows the first two five-note groupings.

Continue the pattern up as far as is comfortable.

Ex.5-46 shows the reversed version of the same two five-note groupings descending by half-steps. Start the pattern as high up as practical and work it all the way down.

### Seven-note groupings

Alternating between three ascending 5th intervals and four descending 4th intervals produces seven-note groupings that climb up by half-steps.

Ex.5-47 shows the first two seven-note groupings.

Continue the pattern up as far as is comfortable. When you get to the top, reverse the order of the notes and work the reversed groupings all the way back down.

# Serial tone-rows, part 3: 23rd chords

You might be wondering what a 23rd chord is. Ordinarily the highest number we see in a chord symbol is 13 because a 13th chord has all seven notes of a scale. In tertian harmony, or harmony by 3rds, we stack 3rds to build chords. If the chord has all seven notes the thirds give us a root, a 3rd, a 5th, a 7th, a 9th, an 11th and a 13th. The 9th is the same note as the 2nd, the 11th is the same note as the 4th, and the 13th is the same note as the 6th. That's all seven notes in an ordinary scale, but in modern music we have an equal-tempered chromatic scale of twelve notes, so more extensions are theoretically possible. A 3rd above the 13th would be the 15th. A 3rd above the 15th would be the 17th. A 3rd above the 17th would be the 19th. A 3rd above the 19th would be the 21st. Finally, a 3rd above the 21st would be the 23rd. A 23rd chord uses all twelve notes, so that really is as far as we can go in a twelve-tone system.

*Lennie Tristano's Dmaj7 over Cmaj7 – introducing the augmented 15th*

Play Ex.5-48.

This is an arpeggio going up a root position Cmaj7 chord and continuing up a root position Dmaj7 chord starting from the 9th above C. This creates the extensions 9th, #11th, 13th, and a #15th. This superimposition was used by pianist Lennie Tristano. Ordinarily a C# would be about the "out-est" or even "wrongest" note for a Cmaj7, but in this context it sounds even "righter" than a natural 15th, or high C natural. This is in part due to the fact that all the 5ths that occur within the arpeggio are perfect 5ths.

Ex.5-49 shows the augmented 15th arpeggio broken into all of its perfect 5ths.

Ex.5-50 is a pattern in triplets demonstrating that the augmented 15th chord is made up of an ascending series of alternating major and minor triads.

*Extending the 15th chord up to the 23rd*

A simple way to find the extensions above the 15th is to figure out the four notes that didn't occur in the 15th chord. On the Cmaj7#15 chord the left over notes are F, Ab, Bb, and Eb, which can be seen as an Fmi7 with a 4th (Bb) replacing the 5th (the note C). In a 23rd chord, however, just as the 15th has the same letter as the root, the 17th has the same letter as the 3rd, the 19th has the same letter as the 5th, the 21st has the same letter as the 7th, and the 23rd has the same letter as the 9th. This would make the "correct" spelling E# (aug17th), G# (aug19th), Bb (min21st), and D# (aug23rd), as shown in ex.8-55. Since we're dealing with twelve-tone music using a notation system based on seven notes, we won't worry too much about "correct" spelling. For instance, the diminished 3rd between the G# and the Bb is harder to read than the easier major

2nd from Ab to Bb. I'll probably use the F-Ab-Bb-Eb spelling. These four notes are the "way outside" part of the chord. They are very dissonant on Cmaj7 and also shatter the earlier series of perfect 5ths and alternating major and minor triads.

*Some lines using the Cmaj7 23rd chord*

One good way to play a twelve-tone arpeggio is to start with the first six ascending notes, then octave-displace the last six notes down. Ex.5-51 demonstrates.

After returning to a C note the entire line is shown in reverse. The following examples will only show the "forward" ascending portion, so it will be up to you to do the reversed versions.

Ex.5-52 divides the twelve into seven-plus-five using the octave-displacement.

Ex.5-53 divides the twelve into five-plus-seven using the octave-displacement.

Ex.5-54 divides the twelve into five-plus-four-plus-three using the octave-displacement.

Ex.5-55 divides the twelve into three-plus-four-plus-five using the octave-displacement.

149

Ex.5-56 divides the twelve into four groups of three using the octave-displacement.

Ex.5-57 divides the twelve into four-plus-three-plus-three-plus-two using the octave-displacement.

Ex.5-58 divides the twelve into five-plus-three-plus-three-plus-one using the octave-displacement.

Ex.5-59 divides the twelve into two-plus-three-plus-three-plus-three-plus-one using the octave-displacement.

Ex.5-60 divides the twelve into six groups of two using the octave-displacement.

The twelve notes of the 23rd arpeggio don't have to be played in strict tertian order. Ex.5-61 shows a line where the "way out" notes are inserted inside portions of the augmented 15th chord.

In Ex.5-62 the "outest" notes are grouped together in the middle of the line and the augmented 15th arpeggio is played out of order as well.

You can continue with your own experiments along this line.

### *A 23rd chord made from the four augmented triads*

Perhaps my own personal favorite 23rd chord consists of the four mutually-exclusive augmented triads whose roots are separated by major 7ths. This chord is all major and minor 3rds (two major, one minor, two major, one minor, etc.). The chord arpeggio has a very wide range in its pure form. Let's check it out.

### *Some lines using the C augmented 23rd chord*

As with the Cmaj7 23rd chord, we can play a C augmented 23rd chord by dividing the twelve into two groups of six using octave-displacement. Ex.5-63 demonstrates.

Ex.5-64 shows the first three 7th chords contained in the C augmented 23rd chord, Cmaj7#5, Emaj7, and G#mi-maj7, the three types of 7th chords found inside the C augmented 23rd chord.

Ex.5-65 shows the first three 9th chords contained in the C augmented 23rd chord, Cmaj7#5#9 , Emaj7#9, and G#mi-maj9, the three types of 9th chords found inside the C augmented 23rd chord.

Ex.5-66 divides the twelve into three groups of four using octave-displacement. The resulting arpeggios spell out Cmaj7#5, Ebmaj7, and F#mi-maj7, three mutually-exclusive 7th chords.

Ex.5-67 divides the twelve into five-plus-seven using the octave-displacement.

151

Ex.5-68 divides the twelve into seven-plus-five using the octave-displacement.

Ex.5-69divides the twelve into four groups of three using the octave-displacement.

Ex.5-70 divides the twelve into four-plus-three-plus-three-plus-two using the octave-displacement.

Ex.5-71 divides the twelve into two-plus-three-plus-three-plus-three-plus-one using the octave-displacement.

Ex.5-72 divides the twelve into five-plus-four-plus-three using the octave-displacement.

Ex.5-73 divides the twelve into three-plus-four-plus-five using the octave-displacement.

Ex.5-74 divides the twelve into six groups of two using the octave-displacement.

152

### A 23rd chord made from the three diminished 7th chords

Another obvious possible 23rd chord consists of the three mutually-exclusive diminished 7th chords whose roots are separated by major 9ths.

### Some lines using the C diminished 23rd chord

As with the other 23rd chords, the C diminished 23rd arpeggio can be played by dividing the twelve into two groups of six using octave-displacement. Ex.5-75 demonstrates.

Ex.5-76 divides the twelve into five-plus-seven using the octave-displacement.

Ex.5-77 divides the twelve into seven-plus-five using the octave-displacement.

Ex.5-78 divides the twelve into five-plus-four-plus-three using the octave-displacement.

Ex.5-79 divides the twelve into three-plus-four-plus-five using the octave-displacement.

Ex.5-80 divides the twelve into four groups of three using the octave-displacement.

Ex.5-81 divides the twelve into six groups of two using the octave-displacement.

I've just shown a few examples to get you started. You should be able to work out many other ways to divide up the twelve notes using octave-displacement.


*The types of 7th and 9th chord arpeggios found inside the C diminished 23rd chord*

It's always a good idea to look inside a large chord (such as a 23ed chord) to see what smaller chords it may contain, giving some clue as to how the whole, or portions, may be applied in specific harmonic situations.

Ex.5-82 shows the four types of 7th chord arpeggios found inside the C diminished 23rd chord.

Of course the first four-note arpeggio is Co7 using an A natural enharmonic instead of the more technically correct Bbb. The next four-note arpeggio is Ebomaj7, followed by what could be called Gbmi-maj7#5. This difficult-to-name chord might also be seen as a first-inversion D major triad with a minor 3rd added on top, or as the top four notes of an Ab13b9#11 chord. Finally there's another difficult-to-name chord that could be called Amaj7sus#5. You might also see it as a second inversion D minor triad with a #4th added on top. If you continue building four-note arpeggios on the higher degrees of the 23rd chord, the same four types of 7th chords will be found again.

Ex.5-83 shows the four types of 9th chord arpeggios found inside the C diminished 23rd chord.

Notice that the four types of 9th chord arpeggios found inside the C diminished 23rd chord are the same as the 7th chords, but each one has a natural 9th added on top. If you continue building five-note arpeggios on the higher degrees of the 23rd chord, the same four types of 9th chords will be found again.


*Another amazing 23rd chord*

There is another amazing 23rd chord that consists of four mutually exclusive triads with (remarkably) all four types of triads represented. That means it has one major triad, one minor triad, one augmented triad, and one diminished triad, and no common tones shared between any of the triads. In the "key" of C this has a root position Cmajor triad on the bottom, a second inversion Eb minor triad above that, then an A augmented triad with a G# diminished triad on top (both in root position).

*Some lines using the new amazing 23rd chord*

As with the previous 23rd chords, the new amazing 23rd arpeggio can be played by dividing the twelve into two groups of six using octave-displacement. Ex.5-84 demonstrates.

Ex.5-85 divides the twelve into five-plus-seven using the octave-displacement.

Ex.5-86 divides the twelve into seven-plus-five using the octave-displacement.

Ex.5-87 divides the twelve into five-plus-four-plus-three using the octave-displacement.

Ex.5-88 divides the twelve into three-plus-four-plus-five using the octave-displacement.

Ex.5-89 divides the twelve into four groups of three using the octave-displacement.

Ex.5-90 divides the twelve into six groups of two using the octave-displacement.

*The types of 7th and 9th chord arpeggios found inside the new amazing 23rd chord*

The amazing new 23rd chord contains all of the interesting types of 7th and 9th chords found inside the diminished 23rd chord, but only one of them repeats as we go on up, so we get even more variety of chord types, just as we had all four types of tertian triads.

Ex.5-91 shows the nine 7th chord arpeggios found inside the amazing new 23rd chord.

On the bottom is a straight C7. Above that we find Eomaj7. Next is the difficult-to-name Gmi-maj7#5, followed by Bbmaj7sus#5, then D#mi7b5, F#mi-maj7, Amaj7#5, another straight dominant, C#7, and finally an Fo7 on top. Some enharmonics are used for the chord spellings.

Ex.5-92 shows the eight 9th chord arpeggios found inside the amazing new 23rd chord.

The eight 9th chords are the same as the 7th chords with three kinds of added 9ths on top, yielding C7#9, Eomaj9, Gmi-maj9#5, Bbmaj7sus#5#9, D#mi9b5, F#mi-maj9, Amaj9#5, and C#7b9. Again some enharmonics. I'll leave it up to you to discover the seven 11th chords and the six 13th chords.

I think that is enough material to keep me practicing for many years to come (hopefully the same for you) so I am going to stop for now. Good luck!

# SHER MUSIC Co. – The finest in Jazz & Latin Publications

## THE NEW REAL BOOK SERIES

## The Standards Real Book (C, Bb or Eb)

A Beautiful Friendship
A Time For Love
Ain't No Sunshine
Alice In Wonderland
All Of You
Alone Together
At Last
Baltimore Oriole
Bess, You Is My Woman
Bluesette
But Not For Me
Close Enough For Love
Crazy He Calls Me
Dancing In The Dark

Days Of Wine And Roses
Dreamsville
Easy To Love
Embraceable You
Falling In Love With Love
From This Moment On
Give Me The Simple Life
Have You Met Miss Jones?
Hey There
I Can't Get Started
I Concentrate On You
I Cover The Waterfront
I Love You
I Loves You Porgy

I Only Have Eyes For You
I'm A Fool To Want You
Indian Summer
It Ain't Necessarily So
It Never Entered My Mind
It's You Or No One
Just One Of Those Things
Love For Sale
Lover, Come Back To Me
The Man I Love
Mr. Lucky
My Funny Valentine
My Heart Stood Still
My Man's Gone Now

Old Folks
On A Clear Day
Our Love Is Here To Stay
'Round Midnight
Secret Love
September In The Rain
Serenade In Blue
Shiny Stockings
Since I Fell For You
So In Love
So Nice (Summer Samba)
Some Other Time
Stormy Weather
The Summer Knows

Summer Night
Summertime
Teach Me Tonight
That Sunday, That Summer
The Girl From Ipanema
Then I'll Be Tired Of You
There's No You
Time On My Hands
'Tis Autumn
Where Or When
Who Cares?
With A Song In My Heart
You Go To My Head
**And Hundreds More!**

## The New Real Book - Volume 1 (C, Bb or Eb)

Angel Eyes
Anthropology
Autumn Leaves
Beautiful Love
Bernie's Tune
Blue Bossa
Blue Daniel
But Beautiful
Chain Of Fools
Chelsea Bridge
Compared To What
Darn That Dream
Desafinado
Early Autumn

Eighty One
E.S.P.
Everything Happens To Me
Feel Like Makin' Love
Footprints
Four
Four On Six
Gee Baby Ain't I Good
To You
Gone With The Wind
Here's That Rainy Day
I Love Lucy
I Mean You
I Should Care

I Thought About You
If I Were A Bell
Imagination
The Island
Jersey Bounce
Joshua
Lady Bird
Like Someone In Love
Little Sunflower
Lush Life
Mercy, Mercy, Mercy
The Midnight Sun
Monk's Mood
Moonlight In Vermont

My Shining Hour
Nature Boy
Nefertiti
Nothing Personal
Oleo
Once I Loved
Out Of This World
Pent Up House
Portrait Of Tracy
Put It Where You Want It
Robbin's Nest
Ruby, My Dear
Satin Doll
Search For Peace

Shaker Song
Skylark
A Sleepin' Bee
Solar
Speak No Evil
St. Thomas
Street Life
Tenderly
These Foolish Things
This Masquerade
Three Views Of A Secret
Waltz For Debby
Willow Weep For Me
**And Many More!**

## The New Real Book Play-Along CDs (For Volume 1)

**CD #1 - Jazz Classics** - Lady Bird, Bouncin' With Bud, Up Jumped Spring, Monk's Mood, Doors, Very Early, Eighty One, Voyage **& More!**

**CD #2 - Choice Standards** - Beautiful Love, Darn That Dream, Moonlight In Vermont, Trieste, My Shining Hour, I Should Care **& More!**

**CD #3 - Pop-Fusion** - Morning Dance, Nothing Personal, La Samba, Hideaway, This Masquerade, Three Views Of A Secret, Rio **& More!**

**World-Class Rhythm Sections,** featuring Mark Levine, Larry Dunlap, Sky Evergreen, Bob Magnusson, Keith Jones, Vince Lateano & Tom Hayashi

## The New Real Book - Volume 2 (C, Bb or Eb)

Afro-Centric
After You've Gone
Along Came Betty
Bessie's Blues
Black Coffee
Blues For Alice
Body And Soul
Bolivia
The Boy Next Door
Bye Bye Blackbird
Cherokee
A Child Is Born
Cold Duck Time
Day By Day

Django
Equinox
Exactly Like You
Falling Grace
Five Hundred Miles High
Freedom Jazz Dance
Giant Steps
Harlem Nocturne
Hi-Fly
Honeysuckle Rose
I Hadn't Anyone 'Til You
I'll Be Around
I'll Get By
Ill Wind

I'm Glad There Is You
Impressions
In Your Own Sweet Way
It's The Talk Of The Town
Jordu
Killer Joe
Lullaby Of The Leaves
Manha De Carneval
The Masquerade Is Over
Memories Of You
Moment's Notice
Mood Indigo
My Ship
Naima

Nica's Dream
Once In A While
Perdido
Rosetta
Sea Journey
Senor Blues
September Song
Seven Steps To Heaven
Silver's Serenade
So Many Stars
Some Other Blues
Song For My Father
Sophisticated Lady
Spain

Stablemates
Stardust
Sweet And Lovely
That's All
There Is No Greater Love
'Til There Was You
Time Remembered
Turn Out The Stars
Unforgettable
While We're Young
Whisper Not
Will You Still Be Mine?
You're Everything
**And Many More!**

## The New Real Book - Volume 3 (C, Bb, Eb or Bass clef)

Actual Proof
Ain't That Peculiar
Almost Like Being In Love
Another Star
Autumn Serenade
Bird Of Beauty
Black Nile
Blue Moon
Butterfly
Caravan
Ceora
Close Your Eyes
Creepin'
Day Dream

Dolphin Dance
Don't Be That Way
Don't Blame Me
Emily
Everything I Have Is Yours
For All We Know
Freedomland
The Gentle Rain
Get Ready
A Ghost Of A Chance
Heat Wave
How Sweet It Is
I Fall In Love Too Easily
I Got It Bad

I Hear A Rhapsody
If You Could See Me Now
In A Mellow Tone
In A Sentimental Mood
Inner Urge
Invitation
The Jitterbug Waltz
Just Friends
Just You, Just Me
Knock On Wood
The Lamp Is Low
Laura
Let's Stay Together
Lonely Woman

Maiden Voyage
Moon And Sand
Moonglow
My Girl
On Green Dolphin Street
Over The Rainbow
Prelude To A Kiss
Respect
Ruby
The Second Time Around
Serenata
The Shadow Of Your Smile
So Near, So Far
Solitude

Speak Like A Child
Spring Is Here
Stairway To The Stars
Star Eyes
Stars Fell On Alabama
Stompin' At The Savoy
Sweet Lorraine
Taking A Chance On Love
This Is New
Too High
(Used To Be A) Cha Cha
When Lights Are Low
You Must Believe In Spring
**And Many More!**

## The All Jazz Real Book

**Over 540 pages of tunes** as recorded by:
Miles, Trane, Bill Evans, Cannonball, Scofield, Brecker, Yellowjackets, Bird, Mulgrew Miller, Kenny Werner, MJQ, McCoy Tyner, Kurt Elling, Brad Mehldau, Don Grolnick, Kenny Garrett, Patitucci, Jerry Bergonzi, Stanley Clarke, Tom Harrell, Herbie Hancock, Horace Silver, Stan Getz, Sonny Rollins, and MORE!

**Includes a free CD of many of the melodies** (featuring Bob Sheppard & Friends.). $44 list price.
Available in C, Bb, Eb

## The European Real Book

An amazing collection of some of the greatest jazz compositions ever recorded! Available in C, Bb and Eb. $40

- Over 100 of Europe's best jazz writers.
- 100% accurate, composer-approved charts.
- 400 pages of fresh, exciting sounds from virtually every country in Europe.
- Sher Music's superior legibility and signature calligraphy makes reading the music easy.

**Listen to FREE MP3 FILES** of many of the songs at **www.shermusic.com!**

See **www.shermusic.com** for more information, including a complete list of tunes in all our fake books.
**To order, call (800) 444-7437 or fax (707) 763-2038**

# SHER MUSIC JAZZ PUBLICATIONS

## The Real Easy Book Vol. 1
### TUNES FOR BEGINNING IMPROVISERS

Published by Sher Music Co. in conjunction with the Stanford Jazz Workshop. $22 list price.

The easiest tunes from Horace Silver, Eddie Harris, Freddie Hubbard, Red Garland, Sonny Rollins, Cedar Walton, Wes Montgomery Cannonball Adderly, etc. Get yourself or your beginning jazz combo sounding good right away with the first fake book ever designed for the beginning improviser.
Available in C, Bb, Eb and Bass Clef.

## The Real Easy Book Vol. 2
### TUNES FOR INTERMEDIATE IMPROVISERS

Published by Sher Music Co. in conjunction with the Stanford Jazz Workshop. Over 240 pages. $29.

The best intermediate-level tunes by: Charlie Parker, John Coltrane, Miles Davis, John Scofield, Sonny Rollins, Horace Silver, Wes Montgomery, Freddie Hubbard, Cal Tjader, Cannonball Adderly, and more! Both volumes feature instructional material tailored for each tune. Perfect for jazz combos!
Available in C, Bb, Eb and Bass Clef.

## The Real Easy Book Vol. 3
### A SHORT HISTORY OF JAZZ

Published by Sher Music Co. in conjunction with the Stanford Jazz Workshop. Over 200 pages. $25.

History text and tunes from all eras and styles of jazz. Perfect for classroom use. Available in C, Bb, Eb and Bass Clef versions.

## The Best of Sher Music Co. Real Books
### 100+ TUNES YOU NEED TO KNOW

A collection of the best-known songs from the world leader in jazz fake books – Sher Music Co.!

Includes songs by: Miles Davis, John Coltrane, Bill Evans, Duke Ellington, Antonio Carlos Jobim, Charlie Parker, John Scofield, Michael Brecker, Weather Report, Horace Silver, Freddie Hubbard, Thelonious Monk, Cannonball Adderley, and many more!

$26. Available in C, Bb, Eb and Bass Clef.

## The Serious Jazz Book II
### THE HARMONIC APPROACH

By Barry Finnerty, Endorsed by: Joe Lovano, Jamey Aebersold, Hubert Laws, Mark Levine, etc.

- A 200 page, exhaustive study of how to master the harmonic content of songs.
- Contains explanations of every possible type of chord that is used in jazz.
- Clear musical examples to help achieve real harmonic control over melodic improvisation.
- For any instrument. $32. Money back gurantee!

## The Serious Jazz Practice Book By Barry Finnerty

A unique and comprehensive plan for mastering the basic building blocks of the jazz language. It takes the most widely-used scales and chords and gives you step-by-step exercises that dissect them into hundreds of cool, useable patterns. Includes CD - $30 list price.

"The book I've been waiting for!" – Randy Brecker.

"The best book of intervallic studies I've ever seen."
– Mark Levine

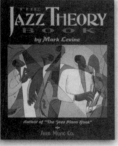

## The Jazz Theory Book

By Mark Levine, the most comprehensive Jazz Theory book ever published! $38 list price.
- Over 500 pages of text and over 750 musical examples.
- Written in the language of the working jazz musician, this book is easy to read and user-friendly. At the same time, it is the most comprehensive study of jazz harmony and theory ever published.
- Mark Levine has worked with Bobby Hutcherson, Cal Tjader, Joe Henderson, Woody Shaw, and many other jazz greats.

## Jazz Piano Masterclass With Mark Levine
### "THE DROP 2 BOOK"

The long-awaited book from the author of "The Jazz Piano Book!" A complete study on how to use "drop 2" chord voicings to create jazz piano magic! 68 pages, plus CD of Mark demonstrating each exercise. $19 list.

"Will make you sound like a real jazz piano player in no time." – Jamey Aebersold

## Metaphors For The Musician
### By Randy Halberstadt

This practical and enlightening book will help any jazz player or vocalist look at music with "new eyes." Designed for any level of player, on any instrument, "Metaphors For The Musician" provides numerous exercises throughout to help the reader turn these concepts into musical reality.

Guaranteed to help you improve your musicianship. 330 pages – $29 list price. Satisfaction guaranteed!

## The Jazz Musicians Guide To Creative Practicing
### By David Berkman

Finally a book to help musicians use their practice time wisely! Covers tune analysis, breaking hard tunes into easy components, how to swing better, tricks to playing fast bebop lines, and much more! 150+pages, plus CD. $29 list.

"Fun to read and bursting with things to do and ponder." – Bob Mintzer

## The 'Real Easy' Ear Training Book
### By Roberta Radley

For all musicians, regardless of instrument or experience, this is the most comprehensive book on "hearing the changes" ever published!
- Covers both beginning and intermediate ear training exercises.
- Music Teachers: You will find this book invaluable in teaching ear training to your students.

Book includes 168 pages of instructional text and musical examples, plus two CDs! $29 list price.

## The Jazz Singer's Guidebook By David Berkman
### A COURSE IN JAZZ HARMONY AND SCAT SINGING FOR THE SERIOUS JAZZ VOCALIST

A clear, step-by-step approach for serious singers who want to improve their grasp of jazz harmony and gain a deeper understanding of music fundamentals.

This book will change how you hear music and make you a better singer, as well as give you the tools to develop your singing in directions you may not have thought possible.

$26 – includes audio CD demonstrating many exercises.

# MORE JAZZ PUBLICATIONS

## The Digital Real Book

On the web

Over 850 downloadable tunes from all the Sher Music Co. fakebooks.

See www.shermusic.com for details.

## Foundation Exercises for Bass

**By Chuck Sher**

A creative approach for any style of music, any level, acoustic or electric bass. Perfect for bass teachers!

Filled with hundreds of exercises to help you master scales, chords, rhythms, hand positions, ear training, reading music, sample bass grooves, creating bass lines on common chord progressions, and much more.

$24

## Jazz Guitar Voicings The Drop 2 Book

**By Randy Vincent**, Everything you need to know to create full chord melody voicings like Jim Hall, Joe Pass, etc. Luscious voicings for chord melody playing based on the "Drop 2" principle of chord voicings.

You will find that this book covers this essential material in a unique way unlike any other guitar book available.

Endorsed by Julian Lage, John Stowell, Larry Koonse, etc.

$25, includes 2 CDs.

## Walking Bassics: The Fundamentals of Jazz Bass Playing

**By swinging NY bassist Ed Fuqua**

**Includes transcriptions of every bass note on accompanying CD** and step-by-step method for constructing solid walking bass lines. $22.

**Endorsed by Eddie Gomez, Jimmy Haslip, John Goldsby, etc.**

## Three-Note Voicings and Beyond

**By Randy Vincent**, A complete guide to the construction and use of every kind of three-note voicing on guitar.

"Randy Vincent is an extraordinary musician. This book illuminates harmonies in the most sensible and transparent way." – **Pat Metheny**

"This book is full of essential information for jazz guitarists at any level. Wonderful!" – **Mike Stern**

194 pages, $28

## Concepts for Bass Soloing

**By Chuck Sher and Marc Johnson**, (bassist with Bill Evans, etc.) The only book ever published that is specifically designed to improve your soloing! $26

- Includes two CDs of Marc Johnson soloing on each exercise
- Transcriptions of bass solos by: Eddie Gomez, John Patitucci, Scott LaFaro, Jimmy Haslip, etc.

"It's a pleasure to encounter a Bass Method so well conceived and executed." – **Steve Swallow**

## The Jazz Piano Book

**By Mark Levine**, Concord recording artist and pianist with Cal Tjader. For beginning to advanced pianists. The only truly comprehensive method ever published! Over 300 pages. $32

**Richie Beirach** –"The best new method book available."

**Hal Galper** – "This is a must!"

**Jamey Aebersold** – "This is an invaluable resource for any pianist."

**James Williams** – "One of the most complete anthologies on jazz piano."

**Also available in Spanish! ¡El Libro del Jazz Piano!**

## The Improvisor's Bass Method

**By Chuck Sher.** A complete method for electric or acoustic bass, plus transcribed solos and bass lines by Mingus, Jaco, Ron Carter, Scott LaFaro, Paul Jackson, Ray Brown, and more! Over 200 pages. $16

**International Society of Bassists** – "Undoubtedly the finest book of its kind."

**Eddie Gomez** – "Informative, readily comprehensible and highly imaginative"

## The Blues Scales

ESSENTIAL TOOLS FOR JAZZ IMPROVISATION

**By Dan Greenblatt**

Great Transcriptions from Miles, Dizzy Gillespie, Lester Young, Oscar Peterson, Dave Sanborn, Michael Brecker and many more, showing how the Blues Scales are actually used in various styles of jazz.

**Accompanying CD** by author Dan Greenblatt and his swinging quartet of New York jazz musicians shows how each exercise should sound. And it also gives the student numerous play-along tracks to practice with. $22

## Essential Grooves

FOR WRITING, PERFORMING AND PRODUCING CONTEMPORARY MUSIC

**By 3 Berklee College professors: Dan Moretti, Matthew Nicholl and Oscar Stagnaro**

- 41 different rhythm section grooves used in Soul, Rock, Motown, Funk, Hip-hop, Jazz, Afro-Cuban, Brazilian, music and more!
- Includes CD and multi-track DVD with audio files to create play-alongs, loops, original music, and more. $24

## Forward Motion

FROM BACH TO BEBOP

A Corrective Approach to Jazz Phrasing

**By Hal Galper**

- Perhaps the most important jazz book in a decade, Forward Motion shows the reader how to create jazz phrases that swing with authentic jazz feeling.
- Hal Galper was pianist with Cannonball Adderley, Phil Woods, Stan Getz, Chet Baker, John Scofield, and many other jazz legends.
- Each exercise available on an interactive website so that the reader can change tempos, loop the exercises, transpose them, etc. $30.

## The World's Greatest Fake Book

Jazz & Fusion Tunes by: **Coltrane, Mingus, Jaco, Chick Corea, Bird, Herbie Hancock, Bill Evans, McCoy, Beirach, Ornette, Wayne Shorter, Zawinul, AND MANY MORE!** $32

**Chick Corea** – "Great for any students of jazz.'

**Dave Liebman** – "The fake book of the 80's."

**George Cables** – "The most carefully conceived fake book I've ever seen."